D1341764

051525

A SAVE–OUR–PLANET BOOK
THE PROFITS GO TO CONSERVATION

TROPICAL FISH
The Rising Generation

WOLFGANG SOMMER

A pair of *Microgeophagus ramirezi* caught in the act of spawning. Photo by H.J. Richter.

Contents

Introduction

WHY DO WE BREED AQUARIUM FISH?

Originally, tropical fish keeping started with the Paradise Fish *(Macropodus opercularis)*, which was imported into Germany in 1869. With its exotic coloration and interesting breeding behavior it created enormous enthusiasm among aquarists and an intensive search for new knowledge. Because of the complicated and difficult transport arrangements required in the early days of tropical fish shipments, each newly imported species became a precious rarity. It was looked after and cared for with respect and dedication. Early literature references document and support this attitude towards newly imported fish. Early aquarists made it an objective of their hobby to breed, if possible, all imported fish—a noble aim which contributed enormously to the development of the aquarium hobby.

There were aquarists, then and now, who earned money and still do so from breeding tropical fish. They, too, have contributed to the growth of the hobby, maybe to an even more significant degree than we can imagine. They, as well as even the smallest hobbyists who are proud of their very first breeding success with tropical fish, have to bring a lot of idealism to the aquarium hobby.

Tropical fish keeping began with the Paradise Fish, *Macropodus opercularis*, which first made its way into the aquarium hobby in the late 1860's. Photo by B. Kahl.

Because the White Cloud Mountain Minnow, *Tanichthys albonubes*, is undemanding in its requirements, it was one of the first fish kept in aquariums. Photo by H.J. Richter.

Before attempting to breed a particular species of tropical fish, such as this *Apistogramma cacatuoides*, the aquarist should obtain as much information as possible about that species. Photo by B. Kahl.

Without idealism neither large-scale breeding nor the dedicated efforts to bring an aquatic rarity to reproduce will succeed. These efforts in the end will begin to fill a gap in our quest for knowledge. A lot of idealism is also required from those aquarists who, at much personal and financial sacrifice, explore the natural habitats of tropical fish, find answers for ecological questions, or discover (or re-discover) a particular fish species and then carry on to breed them.

Because of the current level of technological development, the aquarium hobby is largely capable of supplying most required tropical fish from captive-bred stock. Breeding tropical fish is now common throughout the world, within the hobby as well as in small backyard fish hatcheries, which can meet a substantial quantity of the overall demand for tropical fish. Beyond that, there are large-scale commercial fish hatcheries, especially in Southeast Asia and in Florida. Because of the suitable climate and other favorable conditions in these geographical regions, these facilities can produce tropical fish from throughout the world cost-effectively in large quantities. Let us hope that the efforts to breed tropical fish will receive due recognition and appreciation by those concerned with nature and environmental conservation. This may possibly be the only way to

The Flame Tetra, *Hyphessobrycon flammeus*, is one of a multitude of tropical fish now being bred on commercial fish farms. Photo by B. Kahl.

Glossolepis incisus, the New Guinea Red Rainbowfish, is readily available to the interested hobbyist. Photo by A. Spreinat

The American Flagfish, *Jordanella floridae*, is a native American fish that can be found in well-stocked pet shops. Photo by H.J. Richter.

save certain fish species which are threatened with extinction due to habitat destruction in their native lands. In the final analysis this is an important reason to promote traditionally established tropical fish breeding efforts.

Aquarists will breed fish for the reasons given here, but also with other objectives in mind. Principally, breeding fish has certain challenges. It is in our human nature to show off the recognition received from breeding a "first" or from breeding a particular species. Such success gives us a certain strength and rewards our idealism, the perseverance in our hobby and the love for the individual animal. Being able to breed tropical fish is duly recognized as a high point in tropical fish care. It is essentially a manifestation that the conditions offered in captivity conform largely to the actual requirements of the fish.

WHAT ARE THE PREREQUISITES FOR BREEDING TROPICAL FISH?

Reproduction is the most important function within the life cycle of tropical fish. It commences when suitable environmental conditions occur. In captivity reproduction may not take place when the fish have

Breeding a rarity, such as this *Sturisoma panamense*, is often the high point of tropical fish keeping. Photo by W. Sommer.

been injured, or due to inadequate care of the required environmental conditions. Successful breeding can be evidence of proper care. On the other hand, however, experiences have shown that fish are highly adaptive and can reproduce under less than favorable or less than normal conditions. Inadequacies of this type, however, manifest themselves, for instance, in lower hatching and rearing rates.

If we want to breed aquarium fish, we must ascertain what the optimum requirements are for a particular species and then provide them in captivity. If this is not possible it is advisable to attempt to breed only those fish species which are suitable for particular and available conditions.

The first prerequisite is to thoroughly research all relevant aquarium literature, including *Tropical Fish Hobbyist* magazine, and to talk to experienced aquarists. Deliberate and repetitive breeding of fish is not possible without a suitable foundation of knowledge, to be constantly enhanced with new information.

Beyond that, the breeder has to be able to meet the special and technical requirements. Planned breeding involves more than a single tank. Usually it becomes necessary to temporarily remove the parents, and at times to separate the young from their parents. It is quite possible, though, for fish to breed in a so-called *community tank*, and even a few young can be reared there. If,

A commonly maintained and easy to breed rainbowfish, *Melanotaenia boesemani* is an ideal fish for the beginner. Photo by W. Sommer.

The Desert Goby, *Chlamydogobius eremius*, is a relatively new fish in the world of tropical fish and has proven to be easy to breed. Photo by W. Sommer.

however, a large number of the young are to be raised, the eggs or at least the newly hatched young have to be transferred to a separate tank for special care and attention.

Finally, the evaluation of detailed breeding records or protocols is a further prerequisite for successful tropical fish breeding. Finding quick and easy solutions for particular breeding tasks involves searching for the causes of success or failure with particular breeding attempts.

WHERE DO WE START?

Before attempting to breed a particular species, the aquarist should obtain as much information about that species as possible. He should start by studying the relevant aquarium literature and possibly also geographical reference material in order to obtain sufficient background information about environmental conditions in the natural habitat of that species and its reproductive biology.

Of particular interest from among all prevailing environmental conditions are all chemical, physio-climatic and biological factors which can have an effect on a fish. In particular an aquarist should look for detailed information about the diversity of types of water with their respective water qualities, water temperatures and seasonal variations. In addition, one should look for details about solar radiation, the effects of winds, rainy and dry periods, as well as information about plant growth and the natural availability of food.

A commonly bred tropical fish belonging to the family Cichlidae is *Sciaenochromis fryeri*, also known as the Electric Blue Haplochromis. Photo by B. Kahl.

Nobody, least of all the budding fish breeder, is supposed to be scared off or irritated by the complexity of the environmental factors and conditions and by the suggestions to search for information. Some aquarists, who routinely breed aquarium fish, may well say that things can be much easier and will not hesitate to provide the following proof.

Aquarists commonly breed a variety of tropical fish such as the rainbowfish *Glossolepis incisus* (from Lake Sentani, Western Irian Jaya), the Sturgeon Catfish, *Sturisoma nigrirostrum* (from the Lower Rio Ucayali in Peru), and many of the cichlids of the genera *Julidochromis, Neolamprologus* and *Tropheus* (from Lake Tanganyika in East Africa), very successfully and with high rearing rates in water from municipal water supplies.

Although these breeding successes cannot be argued with, for the aquarist who pursues fish breeding conscientiously and one who is biologically interested, many questions remain unanswered. For instance, why can all these species be bred in water of the same quality? The water quality parameters in the various natural habitats should be compared with those of the municipal drinking water supplies and the differences should be noted. Beyond that we should ascertain what variations in water quality parameters can be

It is useful to keep detailed breeding records of your tropical fish like this *Tropheus duboisi* from Lake Tanganyika. Photo by A. Konings.

Corydoras barbatus caused much excitement when it was first spawned in captivity. Photo by B. Kahl.

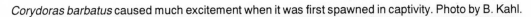

The South American Leaf Fish, *Monocirrhus polycanthus*, needs soft water in order to be bred. Photo by H.J. Richter.

Neolamprologus brevis is one of the many species that can be bred in a wide variety of water quality types. Photo by W. Sommer.

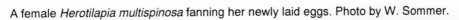

A female *Herotilapia multispinosa* fanning her newly laid eggs. Photo by W. Sommer.

Julidochromis marlieri from Lake Tanganyika is one of best tropical fish for the novice to begin with. Photo by B. Kahl.

tolerated by respective species and where the tolerance limits lie.

When perusing old and new *Tropical Fish Hobbyist* magazines, we may find seemingly contradictory requirements listed for particular species. This often reflects particular breeding experiences, as well as the fact that from one generation to the next a captive-bred species will show a more or less effective adaptation to captive conditions. In effect this means that certain fish species can now be bred in hard water, which was not possible with the originally imported fish or their early progeny.

It is also important for a breeder to know that reproduction in nature is often strongly dependent on changes in environmental factors. It is well known that in our geographical latitudes fish will spawn in spring and summer, seasonally initiated by solar radiation and changes in temperature. Such breeding seasons are also known for many fish in the tropics, i.e., rain forests of South America, Central Africa and Southeast Asia. Tropical fish with reproductive periodicity (periodic breeding cycles) generally spawn during the rainy season, i.e., during rising water levels, change in electrical conductivity (change in salt content of the water), pH and temperature as well as an increase in food supply due to a massive reproduction in plankton. On the other hand, reproductive activity tends to cease during dry periods.

Within the context of reproductive periodicity there are a few recent observations and research results of interest that

Reproduction in nature is strongly dependent on change with fish such as this West African killifish, *Aphyosemion bualanum*. Photo by K. Tanaka.

Reproduction in many species of the elephant-nose fishes, such as *Gnathonemus petersi* **(above),** and Gymnotids like the Green Knifefish, *Eigenmannia virescens* **(below),** are both influenced by changes in the electrical conductivity of the water. Photo above by A. Norman. Photo below by H. Stolz.

are certainly very significant for providing solutions for many breeding objectives. Tests conducted on the Green Knifefish, *Eigenmannia virescens,* and a species of mormyrid, *Pollimyrus isidori,* have shown that regularly changing environmental conditions have an influence over the maturation of sex organs. A continuous increase in electrical conductivity of the water is by itself insufficient to trigger a regressive development of the sex organs. In contrast, decreasing conductivity due to dilution with water containing fewer hardness agents or salt components, respectively, a declining pH and an increase in water level over a period of several weeks, can affect maturation of sex organs and increasing reproductive activities. During the dry season, accompanied by evaporation with a subsequent increase in salinity, there can be a concurrent increase in conductivity of the remaining water. These factors cannot, however, be transposed at random to other fish species and other habitats.

In contrast, it has been shown that minerals dissolved during periods of heavy rainfall can further increase the already increasing conductivity of a particular body of water. This is dependent upon the prevailing geological situation, that is, the soil condition. But equally important is the type of water body. It is obvious that rain and dry periods have a greater influence on small creeks, brooks and generally shallow bodies of water than on large rivers and streams and lakes.

These somewhat comprehensively explained inter-relationships indicate in what detail the aquarist has to study and evaluate the natural habitats of different fish species. Overall, these examples also illustrate that under aquarium conditions with

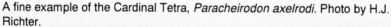

A fine example of the Cardinal Tetra, *Paracheirodon axelrodi.* Photo by H.J. Richter.

Spawning behavior of the Cardinal Tetra, *Paracheirodon axelrodi*, includes a great deal of male and female circling one another. Photos by H.J. Richter.

the usual attempt to maintain water quality, temperature and an optimal food supply, reproduction can indeed be inhibited. At this stage, these discussions should be sufficient to show the significance of understanding environmental conditions and their effect on fish breeding. Points for further discussions will arise in subsequent chapters of this book.

Equally important, though, is a comprehensive knowledge of the reproductive biology of fish. One can assume that, with certain exceptions, specific peculiarities of the reproduction of tropical fish under aquarium conditions have

been documented. We are indebted to the keen observations, diligence, acute sensitivity and perseverance of many fish breeders for important details of the reproductive biology of many aquarium fishes. How else could we have known that breeding Cardinal Tetras, *Paracheirodon axelrodi,* requires extreme cleanliness for setting up the spawning tank, very soft water without carbonate hardness, a weakly acidic pH and keeping the tank dark?

Skilled fish breeders have also observed that breeding the leaf fish *Monocirrhus polyacanthus* requires very soft and, in

The spawning behavior of the Indian glass fish *Parambassis ranga* has been well documented. Photo by W. Sommer.

Only skilled fish breeders should attempt to breed *Monocirrhus polycanthus*. Photo by H.J. Richter.

particular, extremely acid water. In addition, the tiny young of this predatory fish must be fed even smaller fish fry if they are to grow. This is a very labor-intensive process. In fact, about 8 to 10 pairs of Blue Gouramis, *Trichogaster trichopterus*, are required as fish food producers (their own newly hatched young acting as the food source) for the partial rearing of a single Leaf Fish brood. Beyond that, aquarium observations at the microscopic level have shown that the fry of the glass fish *Parambassis ranga* must initially be fed tiny, slow-moving *Diaptomus* nauplii. These nauplii must actually swim in front of the mouths of the young, otherwise the young will not feed at all. As a last example, reference is made to the complicated reproductive biology of some South American and East African seasonal (annual) fishes, such as the

The young of *Trichogaster trichopterus* are often used as live food for other fish. Photo by B. Kahl.

Cynolebias and *Nothobranchius* species. The type and duration of egg development in these species, including storage of the eggs in damp peat moss, was also discovered under aquarium conditions by experimentally inclined fish breeders.

One of many South American killifish, *Cynolebias affinis*, is considered an annual breeder. Photo by J. Kadlec.

In conclusion, it should be pointed out again how important it is, especially for the beginning aquarist, to study specific literature and breeding reports in order to be able to utilize these experiences. But also it cannot be denied that successful fish breeding requires a certain ability to observe and to make the correct decisions at the right time. Not everything can be rigidly passed on in fish breeding, so there are no exact recipes for breeding fish. Even though advice is taken and the experiences of others are utilized, it is the ability of a correct and independent on-the-spot assessment that is absolutely essential.

WE NEED SOME TECHNOLOGY!

Many tropical fish species will spawn even in a community tank. If there are not too many other fish, there is a good plant and or rock cover and sufficient food, generally some of the young will grow up. In species which provide close parental care of the young, such as labyrinth fishes or cichlids, the entire spawn can be

It is important to study most of the available literature about a particular fish before one decides on keeping and breeding it. It is known that lowering the temperature of the aquarium water will trigger these *Corydoras undulatus* to breed. Photo by B. Kahl.

Pelvicachromis pulcher is a popular cichlid that will readily spawn in a community aquarium. Photo by H. Linke.

removed and transferred to another tank with the same water. This enhances the chances for the young to be reared. Immediately this then raises the need for another tank, additional heating and aeration and additional equipment.

Adequate technology can make the work of a fish breeder very much easier and at the same time enhance most every breeding success. The beginning aquarist acts quite correctly when he matches the level of technical support with his breeding objectives, plans properly and buys cost effectively. Experience has shown that with continued breeding activities certain viewpoints and work practices tend to change, which then continuously places different demands on the available

Right: Aquarium stands are important pieces of equipment in the maintenance of an overall set-up. Photo by I. Francais.

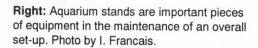

Left: Keeping several aquariums together makes it easier to conveniently work with all the procedures of breeding fish. Illustration by J. Quinn.

technology. Moreover, the space available must always be taken into consideration. To accommodate several breeding tanks, stands or shelves made out of angle iron or lumber are ideal. The enclosed breeding "cupboards," once very fashionable, seem to have gone out of favor. Their advantage, in comparison to open shelves, lies in their heat retention characteristics. When setting up a number of tanks on shelves, on stands or in some other configuration, it is important to calculate the cumulative weight of water and support components, relative to the maximum permissible floor load limits. Water is heavy! It weighs 8¼ pounds per U.S. gallon. The size of breeding tanks depends primarily on the size of species to be bred and on their reproductive behavior. For small tetra and barb species, as well as a large segment of popular killifish and catfish of the genus *Corydoras,* a small breeding tank of about 40 x 30 cm

Placing foam rubber or cork board underneath an aquarium will help to even out any uneven surfaces that may occur on an aquarium stand. Illustration by J. Quinn.

(16 x 12 in.) base size and water level of 25 cm (10 in.) will suffice. Fast-swimming fishes, which usually also engage in very active breeding behavior, require a tank of at least 60 to 80 cm (about 30 in.) long, with the same width and height as mentioned above. Tanks of similar sizes are also suitable for many of the dwarf cichlids and most labyrinth fishes. But anyone who wants to breed large cichlids must utilize substantially larger spawning and rearing tanks. Large fish require more food, their metabolic system produces more waste products which in turn require more frequent water changes. The latter can be an annoyance if the water has to be carried in buckets. Therefore, when setting up a

breeding facility the logistical difficulties must be assessed properly and mitigated with appropriate technical solutions. Automatic water changers are available at most pet shops.

When setting up breeding tanks on an angle-iron stand, it is advantageous to be able to place water storage containers on the highest (top) level. This provides an opportunity to acclimate the water, which, when needed can simply be siphoned into the tanks below. Moreover, it is imperative to have properly conditioned water on hand for sensitive fish fry. As a fundamental rule, water changes are unavoidable, because tank water is subject to a certain ageing process and there is an accumulation of metabolic waste

Power heads can be used to increase the water flow through undergravel filters and are very effective in providing increased water movement and aeration. The power heads shown here are made by the Rolf C. Hagen Corp.

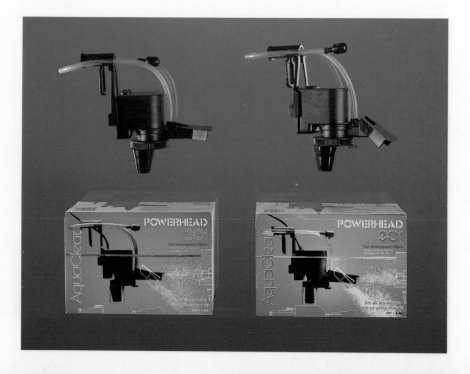

Small fish such as the Threadfin Rainbowfish, *Iriatherina werneri* **(above)**, and *Apistogramma agassizi* **(below)**, require only small aquariums in which to breed. Photos by H.J. Richter.

products. For rearing tanks, at least ¼ to ½ of the entire volume should be changed every second day depending on the particular species and how many are being raised in the tank.

Filtration cannot impede the deterioration of water quality; at best it can delay it. Beyond that, there are a few special hints for the use of filtration in breeding tanks. For small aquariums, a foam (rubber) sponge filter is quite sufficient to provide for aeration and delicate filtration. This type of filtration will not pose a threat whatsoever to newly hatched young, no matter how small they are. It also provides for stable biological filtration, a must for the well being of delicate young fish. If one is concerned about food getting into the filter, one can always turn off the filter during feeding periods. Foam rubber filters should be cleaned *weeky* and adjusted to low flow-through volume.

Filtration for larger breeding tanks, especially when they hold mainly large fish, is easily provided by means of motor-driven canister filters (there are electronically adjustable motor-driven canister filters also). Filters with a high capacity (large water volume turn-over) which produce a strong water current must be avoided. Excessive water flow from a filter can inhibit reproductive activity in some fish. Only careful observation and past experience can determine the best flow-through filter. In order to mitigate strong water flow, the

Some canister filters are designed for positioning outside the tank, but some models, such as the Hagen Fluval 2 model shown here, are used inside the tanks.

The diminutive Chocolate Gourami, *Sphaerichthys osphromenoides*, does not require powerful filtration but instead will function quite nicely with the use of a box or sponge filter. Photo by H.J. Richter.

The Zebra Danio, *Brachydanio rerio*, does not require softened water to encourage spawning. Photo by B. Kahl.

On the other hand, this *Rivulus hartii* does need softened water to stimulate spawning. Photo by W. Sommer.

Running soft water over peat moss will acidify the water enough to the liking of *Apistogramma steindachneri*. Photo by H.J. Richter.

suction and discharge pipe can be covered with a thin layer of foam rubber or nylon mesh.

As a rule, the rearing tank should be filtered mechanically or biologically. The use of chemically acting filter media, such as activated charcoal, should be avoided. This is particularly important when very soft water is used. On the other hand, filtration of soft water over chemically active peat moss is, in certain cases, advisable. Peat moss is capable of binding (removing) a small amount of hardness components and acidifying soft water in a natural way.

Similarly, the use of ozone or UV water sterilizers requires some experience in fish breeding and filtration technology, as well as considerable caution when handling this equipment. Consequently, the beginning aquarist is once again advised strongly to use the proven and trouble-free method of frequent water changes.

In regard to aquarium heating, it need only be said that breeding

Digital thermometers like this Hagen horizontal unit are designed for placement on the outside of the tank. They are easy to read and relatively accurate.

Submersible aquarium heaters, like those designed to hang on the side of the tank and not be submerged, are available in different wattages. The Hagen units shown here include both temperature adjustable and non-adjustable types.

Artificial lighting is usually appropriate for a breeding aquarium unless one decides to keep light-sensitive species. Illustration by J. Quinn.

tanks need thermostatically-controlled heaters. When the tanks are built into a so-called breeding cabinet, correspondingly lower heating capacities are required. But it is important that all equipment conform to required safety standards.

The artificial illumination of breeding tanks has to be sufficiently bright to be able to assess, for brief periods, various details, such as the condition of the eggs, the young, and food availability for the young. On the other hand, it must be possible to darken the spawning tank. Many fish prefer to spawn in a semi-dark tank and in many cases the eggs have to be protected against light.

If there is no substrate in the tank, the bottom glass has to be sprayed black, dark green or dark brown on the outside. Alternatively, the tank can also be placed on a dark bottom panel. If the fish are frightened by their mirror images off the bottom glass panel, it is advisable to place a dark plastic (inert) mat directly onto the bottom.

STANDARDS AND PROCEDURES FOR WATER QUALITY

Water, or more precisely water quality, is of considerable yet rather variable importance for breeding fish; and so this needs to be discussed here at some length. As already mentioned before, there are fish which will only reproduce in water with specific quality parameters. This means that there are only very narrow tolerance limits for variations in pH, hardness components and temperature. These values are essentially based on the experiences of tropical fish breeders. In contrast to this, there are also some fish species which can accept water of variable quality and breed under these conditions without difficulties. When selecting particular species

Cynolebias species *(C. alexandri* above, *C. minimus* below) and other South America "annual" killifish species spawn in much the same manner as African "annual" killies—but the eggs must be treated differently. Photo above by K. Tanaka; photo below by Ed Taylor.

Apistogramma pertensis **(above),** and *Pyrrhulina spilota* **(below),** may accept a wider range of water quality in regard to hardness and pH than many other tropical fish currently available. Photo above by H. Linke; photo below by W. Sommer.

for breeding, the aquarist must make his selection on the basis of these two categories. The available aquarium literature with detailed descriptions of particular species contains sufficient references about their respective requirements in regard to particular water quality parameters.

Both the filter itself and the filtration media used in it affect the quality of the water in a given tank, so reliable brands of filter media like the Hagen filter floss and activated carbon shown here should be used.

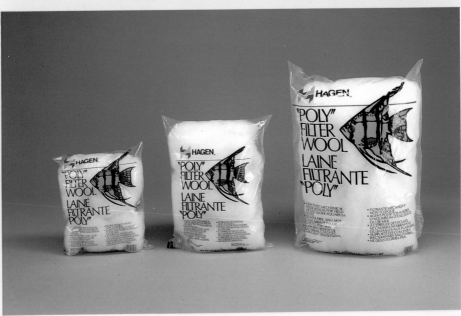

By looking into currently available literature one can readily ascertain that *Labidochromis caeruleus* **(above)** differs markedly in its requirements for breeding from South American *Ancistrus* catfish **(below)**. Top photo by A. Spreinat. Bottom photo by U. Werner.

Another criterion arises from the prevailing quality of municipal drinking water supplies. One makes the assumption that in nearly all cases THE water source is the municipal water supply for the care and breeding of tropical fish. At this point the aquarist has to decide whether to improve the water quality to facilitate the requirements of the fish, or whether he selects fish species which can be bred in the available water.

Anyone attempting to breed fish for the first time is best advised to select the second option; it requires less work and makes caring for the fish easier.

Consequently, it does not make any sense for a breeder who has hard water to stubbornly insist on wanting to breed fish which require water which is soft. Breeding failures are often the result of wrong decisions made at the very start. It is not uncommon for the budding fish breeder to throw up his hands in despair because his own, incorrect decision has robbed him of all further interest in breeding fish. There is no locality where the drinking water supply is so bad that it cannot be used for breeding some fish. Moreover, one can select suitable tolerant fish species for every type of water

Neolamprologus multifasciatus is one tropical fish that can be spawned in nearly all types of municipal water. Photo by W. Sommer.

It would not make much sense to stubbornly insist on breeding soft water-loving fish such as this *Aphyosemion striatum* **(above)** in hard water. *Melanochromis auratus* **(below)** would be a better choice for attempting to breed fish in hard water. Photo above by Elek. Photo below by H.J. Richter.

quality. There are fish, such as egg-laying toothcarps (killifish) and small tetras or barbs, which require only a few liters (quarts) of soft water. For that purpose it is easy to collect rain water, provided the catchment basin or container is clean (letting the rain run off for some time before the water is collected). It must be stated that collected rain water from most industrialized areas of the world is risky, at best. Sheets of plastic suspended from ropes make an excellent catchment basin. A small drainage hole is punched into the center, and a container placed on the floor below collects the rain run off. Since the mineral content of rain water is often extremely low, it should be mixed with 1 to 3% of

These small South American tetras, *Hemigrammus caudovitattus*, require only a small amount of soft water mixed in with straight tap water in order to have a properly conditioned environment. Photo by B. Kahl.

Betta edithae appreciates the addition of soft water in its confines in order to stimulate spawning activity. Photo by H.J. Richter.

tap water. This water is used for spawning and is retained until the young have hatched and started to feed. From then on, with each water change, the tank water is gradually changed over to ever increasing volumes of tap water.

Now a brief discussion on the terminology of water chemistry and detailed suggestions for breeding fish. To start out, the beginning breeder should learn and understand certain terms. A more comprehensive understanding of the complex topic of water chemistry will generally arise from involvement in the practical aspects of fish breeding and the more challenging breeding tasks which an aquarist sets for himself.

From an aquarist's point of view, the most important, without going into great

A gorgeous pair of Central American livebearers, *Limia nigrofasciata*. The males of most livebearers are more gaudily colored than females. H.J. Richter.

Although the Cardinal Tetra, *Paracheirodon axelrodi* **(above)**, and the Butterfly Cichlid, *Anomalochromis thomasi* **(below)**, belong to two separate families, they nonetheless both have similar environmental conditions. Photo above by B. Kahl. Photo below by W. Sommer.

Lamprichthys tanganicanus from Lake Tanganyika is one of the few killifish that requires hard water in which to thrive and breed. Photo by W. Sommer.

detail, are as follows. The more frequently used term water hardness refers in the first instance to total hardness dH (degree of German hardness). It is mainly of importance to water management. Soft water is characterized by a total hardness of 8° dH, medium hard water above 8° dH to 18° dH and hard water in excess of 18° dH. For aquarium purposes in general and for fish breeding in particular we need to know more about this. The total hardness is the sum of the carbonate hardness and non-carbonate hardness. It includes all dissolved alkaline ions or hardness components. Most tropical fish stores and pet shops carry inexpensive test kits (with detailed instructions on how to use them) for measuring total hardness and carbonate hardness. In fact, these kits should be standard tools for any tropical fish breeder since they are sufficiently accurate to provide useful data for most breeding situations. Even buying an electronic conductivity meter does not eliminate the need for further chemical determination, because the conductivity measured gives only an equivalent value for the total salinity and does not provide any details about carbonate and non-carbonate hardness.

The non-carbonate hardness,

These Rosy Barbs, *Puntius conchonius,* can tolerate a wide range of water quality. However, water quality more to their liking will be necessary if one wishes to spawn them in captivity. Photo by H.J. Richter.

Test kits are highly recommended tools for aquarists to use in determining the quality of their aquarium water. *Pseudocrenilabrus philander dispersus* **(above)** will require hard, alkaline water to breed in, while *Austrofundulus limnaeus* **(below)** needs soft, acid water in which to breed. Photo above by H.J. Richter. Photo below by J. Thomerson.

also called retaining or permanent hardness, is made up of the sulfate, chloride, nitrate and phosphate content of calcium and magnesium in the water. The single largest compound is calcium sulfate. According to the latest information available, non-carbonate hardness has no apparent effect on the biological processes involved in reproduction. On the other hand, calcium and magnesium carbonate levels are of importance to breeding tropical fish. The carbonate hardness has a negative effect particularly on the sperm and eggs of fish species from areas with extremely soft water (the Amazon region). Breeding these species normally requires water with a carbonate hardness of less than 3° dH. For most other fish a carbonate hardness from 3° dH to 8° dH is considered to be ideal. The carbonate hardness, in turn, is dependent upon the level of

The carbonate hardness of the aquarium water may have a negative effect on the eggs of soft water fish such as the Flame Tetra, *Hyphessobrycon flammeus*, if it is too hard. Photo by H.J. Richter.

Part of the spawning behavior of *Hyphessobrycon flammeus* entails close body contact. Photo by R. Zukal.

After a great deal of physical contact, eggs are usually scattered among aquatic vegetation. Photo by R. Zukal.

dissolved carbon dioxide (CO_2) in the water. It is able to bring the hard-to-dissolve carbonates into soluble hydrogen carbonates. Therefore, in the aquarium the carbonate hardness components perform an important function as a buffer against another significant factor, the pH value.

The general rule is: the higher the carbonate hardness, the higher the pH value is or the more alkaline the water is. In contrast, the pH value in water with little carbonate hardness and a substantial carbon dioxide content would drop to undesirable low levels; that is the water would become acid. The interdependence between carbonate hardness, carbon dioxide and the pH are of great importance for the aquarium practice. The aquarist should understand the implication of this

A spawning pair of *Hyphessobrycon flammeus* beginning to scatter their eggs. Photo by H.J. Richter.

A number of aquarium products besides pH test kits have a connection with the water's relative acidity/alkalinity. The Hagen Fin Care water conditioner at right buffers the pH of the tank in addition to its other functions, and the Hagen aquarium gravel cleaners shown below remove decaying matter that tends to over-acidify the water.

relationship and its effect of breeding tropical fish. The pH value expresses ratios of hydrogen (H^+) ions to hydroxyl (OH^-) ions, or in other words the relationship between acids and bases in water. If both are present in equal amounts the pH is neutral and is given the numeric value of 7, on a scale from pH 0 to pH 14. When the pH falls below 7, the acid component is larger than the base component (=acidic water), when it rises above 7 the bases become prevalent and we have a basic or alkaline water.

The pH scale is not based on a linear progression but on one that is logarithmic. Therefore, it is important to keep in mind that, for instance, water with a pH of 6 contains ten-times more acid than water with a pH of 7. This then makes it clear that a change of only a single grade can have a profound biological effect. A fish breeder is well advised to make a deliberate pH change only with

the greatest of caution and much consideration. Most good tropical fish shops also carry pH test kits with explicit instructions on how to use them. For quicker and more accurate measurements (and at considerably higher cost!) an electronic pH meter can be purchased from many scientific laboratory supply companies.

A pH value measured does not, however, provide any information about the type of acid or base involved. For instance, a large amount of a very weak acid (humic acid) has the same effect on the pH value as a few drops of a strong acid (phosphoric acid).

When changes in pH have to be made, it is important to do so gradually to allow the fish, like this *Papiliochromis altispinosa*, to safely adjust to the new water chemistry. Photo by W. Sommer.

These Long-finned African Tetras, *Brycinus longipinnis*, are best kept in water with a low hardness and pH. Photo by F. Elias.

This somewhat simplified representation of the chemical processes involved is sufficient for a summary of the essential points which need to be understood for breeding aquarium fishes.

The pH value, by itself, does not have the biological significance it is generally afforded. In natural fish habitats the pH is produced exclusively by the carbonate hardness (basic reaction) and carbon dioxide (acidic reaction). The so-called "black water" regions of South America and Southeast Asia have derived their descriptive name from humic and fulvic acids as a result of the decomposition of plants, which has also given this type of water a weak acidification. These waters are extremely soft, or low on mineral content. In many cases they also display very low pH values (pH 4 to 5).

For the fish breeder it is only of interest to know what substances have made up a particular pH value. Therefore, it is important to remember that the pH should only be modified through the use of a substance which occurs in nature. Biologically it does NOT make sense to increase the acidity of water which has a high carbonate hardness. This would

In regard to this West African cichlid, *Pelvicachromis pulcher*, it is known that improper water hardness and pH will dramatically affect the sex ratio of the young. Photo by W. Sommer.

When the hardness of the water is medium to soft, *Pelvicachromis pulcher* will be more inclined to spawn. Photo: Midori Shobo.

The female *Pelvicachromis pulcher* tending her eggs. Notice how close the female remains to the eggs as they develop . Photo: Midori Shobo.

The newly hatched *Pelvicachromis pulcher* will stay in the vicinity of the spawn site for several days before venturing farther. Photo by M. Shobo.

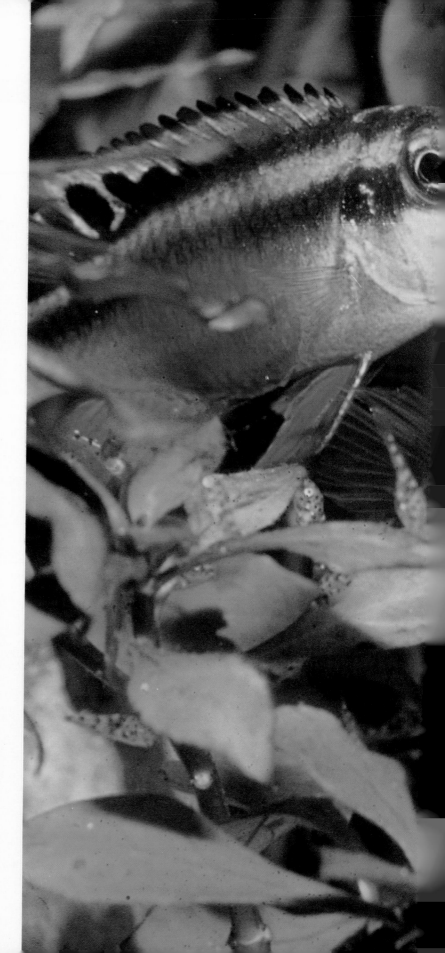

A gaudily colored pair of *Pelvicachromis pulcher* herding their newly hatched young about in search of food. Photo by MP & C Piednoir.

require relatively strong acids. From a fish-breeding perspective, proceeding in such a manner would be meaningless and it would hardly produce a positive reaction among the fish. Anyone wanting to breed fish species from distinct soft water areas who has water of the required quality should only filter this water over high quality, fertilizer-free peat moss or treat it with peat moss extracts. In any event, before using water in a newly set-up breeding tank, it must first be conditioned and heavily aerated before fish are introduced. This treatment stabilizes the tank's pH value.

The breeder must also keep in mind not to transfer fish from water of a particular quality to another one with a different water quality. This is particularly important when changing from mineral-rich to mineral-poor water. Because of the dramatic change in osmotic pressure, the up-take or loss of minerals by the fish's body, tremendous stress is imposed which can harm the fish. If a change in water quality is required the following precautions should be taken. The breeding fish are transferred to another tank with some of the old water (enough for the fish to be able to swim). Then, using an air hose the pre-conditioned (new) water is siphoned into the tank, preferably only drop-by-drop. This gives the fish an opportunity to become gradually acclimated and so will not sustain any harm.

Concluding this chapter on water quality, it must be emphasized once again that the beginning aquarist should initially breed fish in water from municipal drinking water supplies only (adding a name-brand water

Pelvicachromis pulcher will almost always lay their eggs in the secluded protection of a cave. Photo by W. Sommer.

With the discusfish *Symphysodon aequifasciata* it is useful to keep detailed notes on their breeding and fry rearing, simply because their breeding behavior is most fascinating. Photo by B. Degen.

conditioner from your local pet shop). It will then become readily apparent that many fish species can be bred without problems in prevailing water qualities of a medium total hardness and a neutral pH. For that reason a detailed discussion on the treatment of water with ion-exchange resins or by means of reverse osmosis has been omitted in this book.

PLANNED BREEDING—KEEPING RECORDS IS IMPORTANT

Any aquarist who keeps his fish correctly will find that some fish will breed even in a community tank. Nearly all livebearers, many of the popular cichlids, a large number of labyrinth fishes and occasionally even killifish and various small catfish species will breed in the presence of other fish. Sometimes it may require only a few prerequisites that have inadvertently been met to trigger a reproductive response. For cave-brooding cichlids, this means the availability of a small flower pot, a pile of rocks or coconut half-shell. Dwarf gouramies and Siamese fighting fish will easily breed in a quiet corner, well-protected by tall underwater plants. Certain members of the catfish family Loricariidae (well-fed on a vegetarian diet) need nothing more than a bamboo or plastic PVC tube in which to deposit their eggs.

For many substrate-spawning fish, like this *Nanochromis squamiceps*, artificial caves are ideal breeding places. Photo by H. Linke.

Other fish require a plant-filled surface in which to breed and incubate eggs, like these Dwarf Gouramis, *Colisa lalia*. Still others prefer elongate tubing to breed and raise young in, as is the case of the *Ancistrus* catfish below. Photo above by W. Sommer. Photo below by H.J. Franke.

Every aquarist should know in detail the requirements of the fish he or she is keeping. These then should be provided, even in a community tank. The random breedings that may occur under these conditions are valuable experiences for any aquarist, and for many this may trigger the desire to initiate deliberate breeding attempts. Yet, more exciting, stimulating and materially even more satisfying is, of course, a deliberate, well-planned breeding program for specific tropical fish. This leads to the recognition of complex natural history relationships, which promotes observing accurately and, not too infrequently, contributes to the solution of problems in breeding a particular species of fish. Planned breeding commences with reading all relevant articles in hobbyist magazines, aquarium books, the exchange of ideas and experiences with other aquarists, and the preparation of suitable (background) notes. Record all essential information without going into excessive detail. It is recommended to keep records in some sort of short-hand form, possibly on index (3 x 5") cards. This card file increases with the

The males of *Ancistrus* catfish are the ones that tend the eggs once the female has laid them. Photo by H.J. Franke.

Planned breeding commences with reading all relevant articles in hobbyist magazines pertaining to the fish one chooses to breed. Photo above shows a *Rineloricaria* sp. watching over its eggs, while photo below shows the entire fish. Photos by D. Sands.

number of fish that are bred, and it soon becomes a valuable reference source. The following example (for the labyrinthfish *Betta imbellis* LADIGES, 1975) shows the details that may be recorded and the format of such a card file.

BETTA IMBELLIS, Ladiges, 1975
Details summarized from the following literature: PS-874, Hans-Joachim Richter, *Gouramis and Other Anabantoids.*
Lesser Fighting Fish, *imbellis* (Latin) = peaceful, not warrior-like. First described by: LADIGES, 1975.

Range, ecology: Western Malaysia, Malaccan Peninsula (southwestern Malay Peninsula), north and south of Kuala Lumpur (D. Schaller), Phuket Island (S.E. Thailand); water-covered rice paddies, drainage ditches along side rice paddies or in small ponds. Total hardness: 8° to 10° dH, pH neutral (7.0), conductivity 270 to 530 microS, water temperature 34° C (93°F). Found mainly among plants and along overgrown banks. Total Length: about 50 mm, (2") one of the smallest labyrinthfishes.
First importation: 1970 by Schaller, Freiburg, Germany.

A beautiful specimen of *Betta imbellis* in all its glory. Photo by W. Sommer.

INTRODUCTION

Sexual differences: males are dark blue, almost black, with long ventral and large median fins, red margin around caudal fins.

Aquarium maintenance: preferably in pairs only in small tanks from about 20 liters upward. Several pairs only in

During breeding, the male *Betta imbellis* will wrap its body around the female, squeezing out her eggs as his sperms comes out, thereby fertilizing the eggs. The male quickly takes the expelled eggs and places them into the bubblenest to incubate. Photos by W. Sommer.

larger tanks, males rather aggressive, territorial fighting during courtship.

Temperature: 25° to 30°C (77-86°F).

Spawning: about 150 eggs, size 1.05 mm. Duration of egg development to free-swimming stage about 76 hours (26-27° C, 5-6° dH.

First food: must be very small protozoans. *Artemia* nauplii after 5 to 6 days. Rapid growth. Valuable aquarium fish; rarely ever available. Crossing this species with *Betta splendens* produces very attractive hybrids (red veil), which can reproduce (Richter) although hybridization should not be promoted or advocated. This information provided by the book authors is extensive and shows what useful information for breeding particular species can be obtained from relevant literature sources. Therefore, I recommend to any aquarist who wants to breed tropical fish to start setting up his own aquarium library.

It is the male *Betta imbellis* and not the female that watches over the young. Photo by H.J. Richter.

Hybridization of related fish may produce interesting material; however, it should be avoided whenever possible since hobbyists invariably insist on pure-bred stock. Photo above shows a male *Betta splendens* attempting to breed with a female *Macropodus* species. Photo by H.J. Richter.

The Brood Stock

SELECTION AND CARE OF BREEDING STOCK

Once the decision has been made to attempt breeding a particular fish species, it is advisable to purchase 6 to 8 sub-adult or juvenile specimens instead of fully grown adults as pairs. The young must be healthy or at least appear to be so and they must be in excellent condition. This can best be ascertained by watching the fish for a while before actually purchasing them. This is rather important since only vigorously active, robust and healthy fish are suitable for eventual breeding purposes.

If possible, newly acquired fish should be kept in a quarantine tank for one month of initial observation purposes. With optimal care and maintenance the

If one desires to breed a particular species of fish, such as these *Corydoras hastatus*, it is advisable to purchase 6 to 8 juvenile specimens to raise up together. Photo by H.J. Franke.

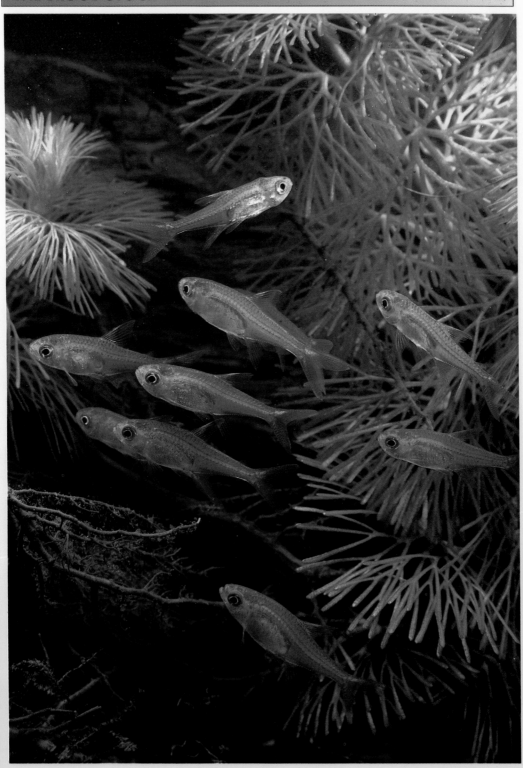

If possible, newly acquired fish such as *Hyphessobrycon amandae* should be kept in a quarantine tank for one month for initial observation purposes. Photo by B. Kahl.

fish will soon show growth, natural behavior and species-specific coloration. As the young fish grow up together it is easy to see how they interact with each other and how eventually harmoniously bonded pairs develop. A randomly matched pair is not necessarily a good breeding pair. It is far better for the pairs to be formed naturally from within a group of siblings or similar sized young from different parents raised up together. This is an old tropical fish breeders' theorem and at the same time it is also the basis for success in fish breeding. In observing fish caring for their young, such as cichlids, it is easy to see that each partner plays a distinct role in the courtship. This extends into a well-developed delineation of responsibilities when caring for the young, during hatching of the eggs, the frequent relocation of the brood and looking after the free-swimming young, to list only a few examples from the overall behavioral pattern. If one of the partners does not conform to its particular role there can be disharmony, fighting and, as frequently happens, the eggs may get eaten. In particular, among rather sensitive Discus cichlids it has

As young fish grow up it is easy to see how they interact with each other, as can be seen in these young discus, *Symphysodon aequifasciata*. Photo by B. Degen.

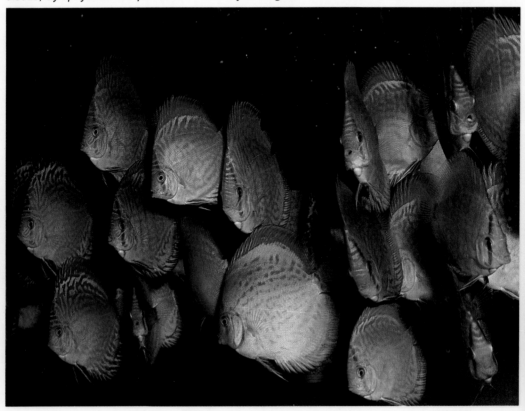

A randomly matched pair is not necessarily a good breeding pair. Instead, it is better for the pairs to be formed naturally from within a group of siblings or similar sized young. Two examples of mated pairs of Discus, *Symphysodon aequifasciata*. Photos by Aqua Life Magazine, Japan.

been demonstrated over and over again that successful breeding only occurs among harmonious pairs. Even with naturally bonded pairs it may take several spawnings until they raise one lot of young successfully. Special Books by Degen, Wattley, Schmidt-Focke and Axelrod should be consulted for information on Discus.

Among non-brood caring fishes it is far more difficult for the observer to determine the specific roles of the partners during breeding. Yet, these experiences about the formation of pairs are also applicable to tetras, barbs and many other species. For instance, courtship behavior among barbs starts within a school. Then individual pairs split off from the school in order to spawn. The strongest and most gravid females are favored by the males. Being closely pursued by the male, they select the spawning site. The actual mating and the discharge of eggs and sperm take place only after prior synchronization and during close body contact. In doing so, the male curls the posterior part of its body around the dorsal fin of the female. This type of spawning, common among *Rasbora heteromorpha*, takes place below

By allowing these Discus *Symphysodon aequifasciata*, to pair off on their own, the end result will be a successful spawning. Photo by A. van den Nieuwenhuizen.

the leaves of water plants. In this position, male and female must function harmoniously in order to act in synchronization during the (up-side-down) mating position. In artificially mated pairs, mating often does not occur. Experienced breeders know that such problems can only be solved by exchanging partners. These two examples are sufficient to point out the advantages of natural pair formation from within a group of siblings.

Once we have a good breeding pair, can we then just keep on breeding them indefinitely ? Apart from the fact that most fish will discontinue breeding intermittently, we must make sure that a breeding pair does get some well-deserved rest. It has to be taken into consideration that in captivity the natural spawning period of most species is out of synchronization with that in the wild. Under aquarium conditions, fish will spawn at different seasons, but only when specific prerequisites have been met. This gives us an opportunity to breed fish when we want to, that is, during autumn and winter months. At other times, during so-called rest periods, we have to cleverly remove the breeding prerequisites. Individual breeding pairs are returned to the group or they are separated for a time of recuperation.

This attractive breeding pair of *Sturisoma nigrirostrum* from South America should be given an occasional rest from breeding so that they may have time to recuperate. Photo by W. Sommer.

During rest periods, the female is sometimes removed or separated from the male by means of a divider in the spawning tank as seen below. These breeding *Pseudocrenilabrus philander dispersus* may require such a separation device. Photo by H.J. Richter. Illustrations by J. Quinn.

A pair of *Epiplatys chaperi* during pre-spawning behavior. These killifish should be given an occasional rest period after several spawnings have taken place. Photo by H.J. Richter.

PREPARATIONS FOR BREEDING

Besides maintaining, increasing, or reducing the diet, the water temperature should be kept at the appropriate temperature, slightly raised or lowered, depending on what your fish require and make fewer water changes again, depending on your fishes specific needs. An initial fasting period is deliberate and has nothing to do with neglecting proper care. Fish also encounter similar periods in the wild, but there they may extend over many weeks when there may not be any food available at all. Collecting totally emaciated wild fish in the tropics during periods of drought have documented this fact repeatedly.

Breeders must pay particular attention to the condition of females. The developing of eggs and the periodic maturation of egg cells are the essential prerequisites for reproduction. Breeding is only possible when the ovaries contain fully developed eggs. When the fish are properly fed, the developing eggs become evident from a gradual bulging of the female's abdominal region. Such females must be afforded the opportunity to spawn, otherwise they may become egg-bound (hardening of egg mass) and are then unsuitable for further breeding. For some fish species it is important that they are permitted to get rid of all eggs. Others spawn intermittently over a period of several weeks. Even if no further young are wanted, the breeding pair should be afforded the opportunity to spawn.

Periodically depriving one's fish of food to clean out the system will help to maintain the health of the fish, much as it does in humans. These White Cloud Mountain Minnows, *Tanichthys albonubes*, should be given periodic fastings in order to cleanse their systems. Photo by H.J. Richter.

The egg-laden female of this pair of pencilfish, *Nannostomus eques*, should be afforded the opportunity to breed, otherwise she may become terminally eggbound. Photo by H.J. Richter.

WHERE, WHEN AND HOW OFTEN DO TROPICAL FISH SPAWN?

Every fish breeder faces these brief yet very complex questions every time he or she wants to breed another species. It is impossible to answer these questions for a large number of species, and it would undermine the independence which every breeder should achieve. These questions can be answered by reading relevant aquarium literature by referring to your own breeding records, notes and observations, and by proceeding with deliberation and thorough forethought.

Perusing the relevant aquarium literature, the reader will quickly discover that not every species is discussed in sufficient detail to give enough breeding information. Quite often there is a passing reference: *For breeding details refer to description of the genus.* For practical purposes this information is often adequate for breeding a particular species. This encourages the breeder to apply this information to other fish species. If we compare, for instance, frequently offered breeding suggestions for bottom substrate spawning, so-called egg-laying toothcarps (killifish), there

Information on breeding killifish of the genus *Cynolebias* is usually applicable to most of the species of that genus, such as this *Cynolebias whitei*. Photo by W. Sommer.

A male *Cynolebias whitei* preparing to breed with a receptive female. Photo by H.J. Richter.

This egg-laden female *Cynolebias whitei* is ready to breed, as can be seen from her swollen appearance. Photo by H.J. Richter.

A pair of *Cynolebias whitei* breeding in the aquatic vegetation. Notice how thoroughly enmeshed they can become in the vegetation. Photo by W. Somme

are indeed common denominators for the South American genera *Cynolebias* and *Pterolebias.* But there are also parallels to the bottom spawning species of the African killifish genera *Nothobranchius, Roloffia* (considered by most workers to be a synonym of *Aphyosemion)* and *Aphyosemion.* From the latter we know that some fish will spawn either on the bottom or attach their eggs to plants, depending upon particular situations. Our initial question provides us with sufficient background information that, for starters, we would provide our fish with a peat moss covered bottom for spawning. Yet, for storing the eggs in peat moss and for the period of egg development the literature provides rather diverse suggestions. The eggs of some species kept in damp peat moss develop in 3 to 6 months. In contrast, the eggs of bottom

spawners and those that attach their eggs to plants develop in about 12 to 20 days and they need not be removed from water and kept in a damp medium. The reasons for these differences in nature can probably be found in the fact that certain water bodies dry out annually for several months *(Cynolebias, Pterolebias*— long periods for eggs to develop). The habitats for bottom spawners and those attaching their eggs to plants do not completely dry out in their native lands.

Returning to the originally posed questions, here are a few more problems. Cichlids which may have spawned in a well-planted community tank often will not breed when transferred into a separate breeding tank. Some of the reasons for this may well be different lighting, less plant cover or the absence of other fish. In order to avoid that, some breeders will keep their breeding stock temporarily in larger groups and in tanks without bottom substrate, plants and other hiding places. Transferring the fish back into the original breeding tank

Killifish eggs of the genus *Cynolebias* require that the eggs be stored in damp peat moss for long periods of time in order to develop properly. Photo at left of *Cynolebias heloplites* by H.J. Rosler. On facing page, photo above of *Cynolebias constanciae* by H.J. Richter. Photo below of *Cynolebias dolichopterus* by H.J. Richter.

with its now improved conditions generally favors spawning willingness.

Once we know the conditions under which particular fish species prefer to spawn, we should attempt to provide these. For instance, various South American catfish *(Rineloricaria, Ancistrus)* would appreciate narrow spawning tubes and gently flowing water. For some cichlids these are flat stones for the eggs to be deposited on, and for cave-brooders an artificial rock cave or a flower-pot substitute. Spawning prerequisites may also include the bottom substrate for digging as well as dense snail shells for the popular snail cichlids of the genera *Neolamprologus* and *Telmatochromis*. Similarly, some fish require bushy water plants *(Myriophyllum, Nitella, Cabomba)* and sometimes even plants with

Once the conditions under which particular fish species prefer to spawn are known, such materials should be provided, as a piece of bamboo or PVC piping for certain suckermouth catfish like this *Rineloricaria microlepidogaster*. Photo by R. Zukal.

A helpful spawning prerequisite for the Lake Tanganyikan shell-dweller *Neolamprologus ocellatus* can be small snail shells. On the other hand, some fish may require bushy water plants like *Myriophyllum hippuroides* in which to lay their eggs. Photo above by A. Konings. Photo below by R. Zukal.

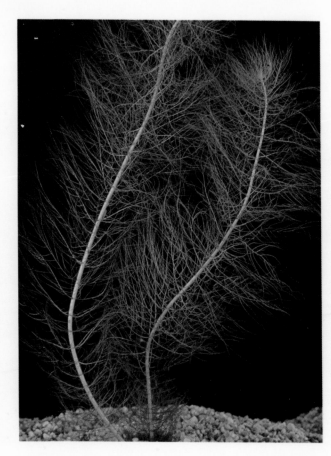

large leaves *(Echinodorus, Cryptocoryne)*, as well as synthetic wool substrates for tetras, barbs, killifish and rainbow fish. Bubble nest-building labyrinth fishes prefer to use floating plants *(Riccia, Salvinia, Pistia)* for their nest building activities.

The essential requirements when breeding fish are practicality and appropriate hygiene and NOT aesthetic considerations. This approach also justifies, in many cases, omission of bottom substrates in tanks used for breeding very sensitive and demanding fish species. There is no other way to guarantee the meticulous cleanliness required for breeding Cardinal Tetras, for instance.

Some of the larger catfish species, such as *Sturisoma* and *Farlowella* species, which feed only on the bottom and which must be given a vegetarian dietary supplement to reach spawning condition, are also best kept in a tank without substrate.

WHEN DO FISH SPAWN AND AT WHAT TIME?

Most species prefer to spawn in the morning, that is, before midday. For that reason, most breeding pairs are introduced into the breeding tank the night before. Firstly, this allows the fish to settle down during the night, and secondly, there is still time to make any adjustments to the water quality and/or temperature.

Large leafy water plants like this *Echinodorus* sp. make ideal spawning mediums for small cichlids and leaf fish.

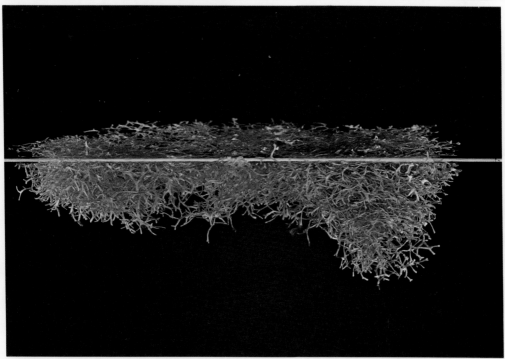

The floating aquatic plant *Riccia fluitans* is ideal for labyrinth fish to construct their bubble nests into. Photo by R. Zukal.

This will often stimulate the fish into spawning immediately the next morning, and is particularly applicable to tetras and barbs. Rainbowfish, too, usually spawn during the early morning hours. With cichlids, it may take several weeks to settle in and feel secure enough to even consider breeding. If they are kept in a community tank, one can often see males courting females right after the tank lights have been turned on in the morning or anytime throughout the day, to be followed by actual spawning later on.

Certain tetras, such as Cardinal Tetras, *Paracheirodon axelrodi*, and Copper Tetras, *Hemigrammus nanus*, are true dusk or night spawners. The adult pair can be placed into the spawning tank during the day, but spawning as such is sometimes delayed for some time (e.g., Cardinal Tetras). In any event, it is advisable to keep the spawning tank dark. The rather attractive Blunt-nosed Gar, *Ctenolucius hujeta*, also prefers to spawn during late evening hours. Yet, once spawning commences the fish are not distracted when the tank illumination is turned on again to watch the fish spawn.

Most killifish will spawn at any time of the day, when male and female (previously kept separate) are introduced into the spawning tank. Similarly, labyrinth fishes do not seem to be tied to a particular time of day. Among cichlids it is common to observe spawning during the afternoon, without being restricted to a particular time. Breeding times seem to be of least importance to livebearers. They will drop their fully developed young at any time of the day.

The question that now remains to be answered is the one about spawning frequency. Hobbyists could be inclined to categorize fish into those that spawn once, several times or constantly. Single spawners are usually those species which spawn only once or twice a year, but then produce a large number of eggs. Most species are repeat spawners, exhibiting a regular spawning rhythm. Within a longer lasting spawning period, these species will spawn repeatedly in intervals of several days or weeks. The number of eggs deposited at each spawning is clearly less than those for species which spawn only once, but the aggregate number of eggs from all intermittent spawnings may be much higher. For some of these fish we recognize periods of greater willingness to spawn within 3 to 4 days of any previous spawning, but most require 5 to 8

The Blunt-nosed Gar, *Ctenolucius hujeta*, prefers to spawn in the late evening hours. Photo by W. Sommer.

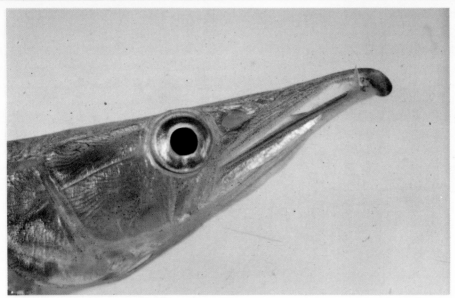

A close-up of the head of the Blunt-nosed Gar, *Ctenolucius hujeta*. Photo by Dr. Herbert R. Axelrod.

Julidochromis ornatus from Lake Tanganyika frequently spawns every 5 to 8 days over long periods of time. Photo by H.J. Richter.

A spectacular school of Cardinal Tetras, *Paracheirodon axelrodi*. Photo by B. Kahl.

days until they are ready to spawn again. Obviously, the time required for eggs to mature is sometimes relatively short. This is clearly influenced by the diet and the prevailing tank water conditions. It should be monitored and controlled, based on precise observations made by the breeder.

In order to achieve good breeding results, a breeding pair of fish must be permitted to spawn at regular intervals. The breeder must know and maintain the spawning cycle of his fish. This is usually accomplished by leaving the fish alone and not interfering or constantly annoying them. If this cannot be achieved, the number of eggs and their fertility rate will decline. If breeding is inhibited altogether, the female, as already mentioned before, can become egg-bound. Apart from short spawning cycles (3 to 4 days and 5 to 8 days) there are fish species which spawn in 8 to 12 day, or 12 to 15 day intervals, or even longer.

How do we recognize imminent spawning in fish? Firstly, by the abdominal shape of the female and, secondly, by the behavior of males and females together. It is usually the male who starts by actively courting the female, often accompanied by an increase in color intensity. In fact, many fish even display a specific breeding coloration.

This male *Apistogrammoides pucallpaensis* is showing off brighter than normal coloration because he is in breeding condition. Photo by H.J. Richter.

The male *Apistogrammoides pucallpaensis* gaurding the periphery of the spawning site while the female tends to other business. Photo by H.J. Richter.

By allowing this *Apistogrammoides pucallpaensis* to care for her eggs and young, a good hatch rate and fry survival is likely. Photo by H. Linke.

If males and females are being kept under the same conditions, one can assume that both partners reach sexual maturity at the same time. Clearly, feeding a quality, balanced diet (live foods, insects and their larva, etc.) has favorable influence on the formation of sex products. Therefore, the breeder should attempt to provide a preponderance of live foods in their diet, such as mosquito larva, fly pupae, and fruit flies *(Drosophila)*. *Daphnia,* blackworms, tubifex worms and *Artemia* are also excellent. The often recommended use of white worms (Enchytrae) tends to make females very quickly too fat.

Continuously spawning fish include those species which lay a small number of eggs every day, over a period of several weeks. Typical representatives of this group are rainbowfish and White Cloud Mountain Minnows. Those considered to be permanent spawners are the Congo Tetra, *Phenacogrammus interruptus,* and Long-finned African Tetra, *Brycinus longipinnis.* Spawning in these two species extends over

The Congo Tetra, *Phenacogrammus interruptus*, considered to be a permanent spawner, will lay small numbers of eggs every week throughout its adult life.

Melanotaenia lacustris **(above)** and *Melanotaenia boesemani* **(below)** also practice permanent spawning. Photo above by H. Bleher. Photo below by H.J. Richter.

several days, whereby a small number of eggs are deposited every day. Such an extended breeding period, however, is followed by a long pause. This shows that even among those fish considered to be permanent spawners there are differences in periodicity and duration of breeding periods.

Nearly all egg-laying toothcarps (killifish) deposit their eggs over a prolonged period, and so many aquarists breed these fish (which spawn on the bottom or attach their eggs to plant leaves or artificial spawning 'mops') more or less permanently. One male is kept with two females for 2 to 3 weeks in a tank with peat moss as a substrate (annual species) or artificial spawning mops (non-annual species) and a balanced diet. The spawning mops can be exchanged frequently or the eggs removed. The peat moss is poured through a fine strainer and the eggs are maintained for their development in slightly damp peat moss.

Brood-caring species do not need special consideration in regard to spawning periodicity and egg maturity. Imminent

The best arrangement for spawning *Aphyosemion australe* is to house one male with two or three females. Photo by W. Sommer.

A spawning pair of Lemon Cichlids, *Neolamprologus leleupi*. Photo by H.J. Richter.

spawning becomes quite evident through conspicuous courtship behavior, preparing a spawning and nest site and the presence of distinct (bright) breeding coloration. Yet, even in some of these species there can be periods of repeated spawnings within certain time intervals. A very interesting combination of several spawnings with continued brood care occurs in several cichlid genera *(Julidochromis, Neolamprologus* and *Telmatochromis)* from Lake Tanganyika. These fish will raise their young from several spawnings in a single large family unit without any problems.

Among the livebearing fishes,

virtually all guppies, swordtails, platies, goodeids, and halfbeaks can produce young throughout the year. The gestation period varies among the species. It lasts at least 3 weeks and can be influenced by external factors, such as temperature and diet.

PREPARATIONS FOR BREEDING

Correct preparation for breeding tropical fish, particularly for the breeding/spawning tank and the treatment or conditioning of the water, requires considerable care and planning on the part of the breeder. Maintaining maximum

The gestation period for livebearers such as this *Xiphophorus maculatus* lasts for about three weeks at a temperature of 78 to 80° F. Photo by L. Wischnath.

The halfbeak *Hemirhamphodon pogonognathus* requires clean aquarium water in order to breed. Photo by M. Brembach.

cleanliness is of paramount importance. The eggs of most fish are very sensitive to chemical and bacterial influences, and so these must be kept to a minimum.

First, the spawning tank must be very thoroughly cleaned. This is best done with clean tap water. Additives, such as dish washing detergents must never be used (they are toxic!), but the very last rinse can contain a 3% solution of hydrogen peroxide.

Tap water or water from a natural spring can be used directly for breeding fish. However, it will need to be dechlorinated using any readily available dechlorinization product from your local pet dealer. The water quality in the breeding tank must conform to the requirements of the species to be bred. The pH must be measured frequently, particularly when very soft water is used. In order to prevent an uncontrollable drop in pH, it is

advisable to add to very soft water some tap water containing carbonate hardness. If fish from black water areas are to be bred, the water can be filtered over peat moss; this must be of highest aquarium quality (originated from elevated, dried-out peat bogs); about 1 liter of peat moss/100L water. Filtration over peat moss reduces water hardness and at the same time it slightly acidifies the water. The water prior to peat moss filtration should have a carbonate hardness of 3° to 4° dH. Tropical fish shops usually sell peat moss extracts as additives for breeding tank water. If used on a small scale and within the directions provided, these extracts can be quite useful and approximate the results obtainable with peat moss filtration. In any event, it is advisable to prepare a large volume of breeding water in order to maintain an adequate supply for later usage. This then provides make-up water for several successive breedings under identical water quality conditions.

If not absolutely necessary, all bottom substrate should be omitted. In order to protect eggs which have fallen to the bottom (from predation), the entire bottom can be covered with pebbles or glass marbles the size of cherries, or, better yet, a plastic spawning grate.

Plants for free-spawning fish should be carefully rinsed off under running tap water. Some of the most suitable spawning plants are *Myriophyllum, Cabomba*, Java moss, *Najas* or other 'bushy' plants, unless broad-leaf plants are required for particular fish. Artificial spawning mops (synthetic wool) are useful also.

Preparing to breed a particular species also includes gathering all the facts about the natural habitat of that species and the prevailing climatic conditions. This applies particularly to the breeding season and possible

Cabomba australis is a good water plant for free-spawning fish to lay their eggs in. Photo by R. Zukal.

Limnophila aquatica is another excellent water plant for the eggs of free-spawning fish. Photo by R. Zukal.

spawning rhythms. These aspects are especially important for newly imported fish, which retain their normal breeding cycle. Yet, for the domesticated progeny of imported fish, that is, well-established aquarium stock, seasonal breeding seasons no longer exist. The breeding seasons for most wild caught tropical fish fall into the months of October through December and February to May.

HOW TO INDUCE SPAWNING

Among tropical fish breeders there are different view points and methods for initiating spawning. Stimulating factors introduced by the aquarist always affect fish, in conjuction with all other environmental influences. Therefore, it is important not to proceed aimlessly but instead to apply, step-by-step, well-thought-out methods in order to trigger spawning. The aquarist must have an opportunity to assess and record the effects of individual stimuli. Only after one factor has failed should a second one be applied or both applied simultaneously. The breeder must

With substrate-spawning cichlids like this *Herichthys labiatus*, the female will proceed to clean the surface of the object she intends to lay her eggs on. Photo by R. Stawikowski.

After the surface of the rock has been cleaned, the eggs are deposited soon thereafter. Photo by R. Stawikowski.

The result of a successful spawning effort by *Herichthys labiatus* is this impressive group of newly hatched young. Photo by R. Stawikowski.

work out for each species suitable methods for breeding. Here are some proven methods to stimulate spawning.

NUTRITION

Without doubt, a correct diet is the single-most decisive factor for obtaining satisfactory breeding results. Keep in mind that the ova in certain species will only mature when a specific type of food is given. Some tetras, such as the Congo Tetra, Long-finned Tetra and Hatchet Fish need insects or insect larva; certain catfish and the Spotted Headstander, *Chilodus punctatus*, require a large amount of plant matter in their diet. Some cichlids from Lake Tangayika, such as *Neolamprologus ocellatus*, *N. brevis* and *N. calliurus*, will only spawn over long periods when provided with a consistent supply of high protein foods in their diet.

A variable yet nutritionally balanced diet is mandatory for

Because the Spotted Headstander, *Chilodus punctatus,* is an herbivore, it will not hesitate to nibble on aquarium plants. Photo by H.J. Franke.

These shell-dwelling cichlids, *Neolamprologus brevis* **(above)** and *Neolamprologus calliurus* **(below)**, need feedings of protein in order to produce large, continuous spawns. Photo above by H.W. Dieckhoff. Photo below by W. Sommer.

A stunning male *Aulonocara jacobfreibergi* from Lake Malawi. Photo by A. Konings.

Xenotilapia flavipinnis is one of the most peaceful cichlids known. Photo by H.J. Richter.

breeding to take place. Certain types of food, required for the maturation of gonads, are given as specific supplements. The aquarists should take his or her time when feeding to observe how eagerly the food is taken and whether eggs are being formed. Even though the value of live food is desirable, the aquarist can further supplement the diet with commercially available, nutritious name-brand dry foods such as pellets, flakes, and freeze dried plankton, which has the advantage of not containing disease carriers. As has been mentioned before, a specifically adjusted diet is highly effective in promoting breeding.

It is important to gauge just how much food one's fish will eat within a 15-minute period. Any food left over after that time usually indicates that too much food has been given.

A wide variety of both live and prepared foods is recommended for these Red-eye Tetras, *Moenkhausia sanctaefilomenae*. Photo by B. Kahl.

A number of specialized devices designed to aid aquarists in removing accumulated wastes from aquaria are available at pet shops. The Hagen Multi Vac battery powered aquarium cleaner is shown here.

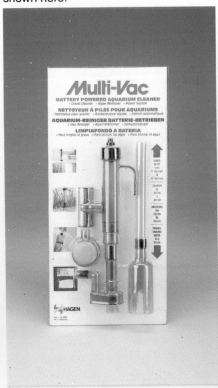

WATER CHANGE

Changing water is an equally important factor for triggering spawning (although not always necessary). There are several methods which can be outlined as follows:

1) A general water change, or, transferring the breeding pair into water of different quality parameters. The method of adding water has already been discussed.

2) The exchange of water in the breeding tank with water of the same quality within a one week period. For fish with a regular spawning rhythm, up to ⅓ of the water is exchanged daily. At the same time accumulated waste products are also siphoned off the bottom. Colder or warmer water can be used for replenishing, and the hardness can be adjusted at

the same time depending on the species. If spawning does not occur, the same procedure is repeated again after a short period. Feeding is continued between water changes. Automatic water changers are available from most pet stores.

3) The most expensive procedure is continuous water changing over a prolonged period of time to simulate the rainy season. It is used for fish which spawn only periodically in the rainy season. This has been observed while breeding the Green Knifefish, *Eigenmannia virescens*. It is possible that many species are subject to such reproductive periodicity. The most interesting aspect of this phenomenon is the proven regression of the sex organs outside the breeding season. When using this method it is important to lower slowly but continuously the hardness (reduction of electrical conductivity) by means of changing water, to raise the water level gradually and to weakly acidify the water by filtering it over peat moss. This requires relatively involved technical facilities. No doubt, there are a number of modifications to these basic methods of changing water

Lowering the hardness of the water may help to induce spawning in many species of knifefish, such as the Black Ghost, *Apteronotus albifrons*. Photo by H.J. Richter.

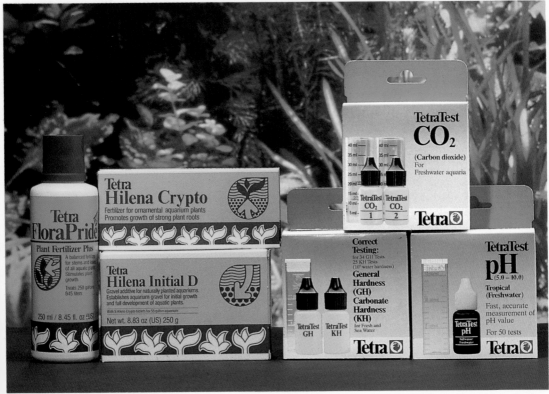

Test kits can help the aquarist monitor a number of different areas of water quality; the three Tetra test kits at right, for example, monitor water hardness pH level and carbon dioxide level.

being practiced among aquarists. For the individual it is, however, important to combine these methods correctly, to record their effect and to evaluate the results.

CHANGING THE PH VALUE

Breeding experiences have shown that all species from waters with a high pH value (e.g., Lake Tanganyika) can also be bred in water with a neutral pH. While there have been breeding experiments where the pH had been clearly elevated above neutral, it has been shown that such adjustments are generally not required. Therefore, when the pH has to be altered downwards,

it should only be a weak acidification by means of peat moss filtration. It is possible that the humic and fulvic acids do not act directly via the pH but instead affect the fish's body in some other form.

In summary, it can be expected that a change in pH is not a significant factor in triggering reproductive activity. Nevertheless, weakly acidic water (pH 6.5 to 6.0) is beneficial for non-alkaline loving species, because it strongly inhibits the development of fungi and protozoans which can harm fish eggs.

TEMPERATURE CHANGE

Temperature is relatively significant for spawning. It is intuitively obvious that tetras from shaded tropical rain forest streams spawn at lower temperatures than labyrinth fishes which use sun-soaked rice paddies for breeding. This must be taken into consideration for general aquarium maintenance as well as for breeding. A change in temperature becomes a factor in reproduction when the breeding pair has been kept under less than optimal temperature conditions prior to breeding.

In most cases a temperature **increase** should be appropriate to contribute to the onset of breeding. On the other hand, a drop in temperature can have a favorable effect on those fish species which spawn during typical rainy seasons. In the wild, fish are exposed to seasonal as well as to day–night temperature fluctuations. Simulating temperature fluctuations as per time of day has found limited acceptance since it may have beneficial effects on the general well-being of fish. The heater is generally coupled to a time switch or is operated in conjunction with a lighting timer. The temperature fluctuation for a standard community tank should be about 2 to 3° C in a breeding tank. A drop in temperature with a simultaneous change of water is, in many cases, one of the best methods to trigger spawning.

A slight increase in water temperature will help to stimulate this male *Trichogaster trichopterus* to breed. Part of the breeding act entails the male's wrapping his body firmly around the body of the female. Photo by H.J. Richter.

In both photos, the male proceeds to encircle the female to initiate the actual spawning. Photos by H.J. Richter.

Rearing the Young

AFTER SPAWNING HAS TAKEN PLACE

It is tempting to say that once the eggs have been laid the breeding pair has done its deed! But that is not always the case. The adults must continue to be cared for as before. Moreover, if the fish are to be used for further breeding the adults must be treated properly and fed well in preparation for the next breeding.

DEVELOPMENT OF EGGS AND YOUNG

Eggs develop from the original egg cells inside the ovary of females. These original egg cells take nutrients from the female's body and store them in the form of yolk. This phase of yolk storage or egg formation can often be seen externally on the female by the increase in abdominal size. Depending upon the species, the

A pair of *Aphyosemion gardneri* about to spawn. Photo by N. Elder.

The male snuggles up close to the female's body in order to fertilize the eggs as they are laid. Photo by N. Elder.

eggs mature in batches, at variable time intervals. This leads to the spawning rhythms or spawning periods, respectively. The time required for maturation of eggs at different stages of development can, for instance, in tetras be only a few days, but for many cichlids it may be several weeks.

We know that eggs are laid only when certain spawning prerequisites are met. If an impending spawning is inhibited by negative external influences, fertility decreases rapidly. As the egg matures a shell protects it on the outside. The egg shell consists of a thick internal membrane (the cortical membrane), and an external mucus membrane. The egg shells contain a tiny opening, the micropyle, which assures admission of the motile sperm into the egg.

Once the eggs have left the female's body, they lose their fertility in a relatively short period of time. In some species this is further enhanced by a strong swelling of the entire egg. Development of an egg shell is highly variable. In many killifish it is thick and hard, so that the eggs can actually be picked up without damaging them. Then there are also eggs which have ray-like projections all around them or long thread-like appendages (e.g., some rainbow fishes). The number

The tough membrane encompassing these eggs helps to protect them from damage. Photo by W. Sommer.

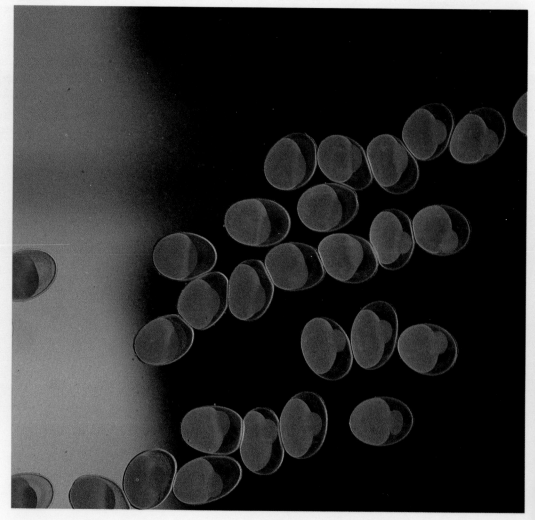

While some fish may produce several hundred eggs per spawning, *Tropheus brichardi* produces only approximately 20 eggs. Photo by A. Konings.

of eggs per spawning is rather variable. Within about 2 hours and after 15 to 20 matings, the Blunt-nosed Gar, *Ctenolucius hujeta*, deposits more than 2,000 small eggs (with a diameter about 1 mm). On the other hand, the mouth-brooding *Tropheus* species have at the most about 20 eggs per spawning, usually less, which have a diameter of nearly 5 mm. (There are about 25 mm in one inch.)

Similar to eggs, sperm develop

over several stages, from single-celled sperm cells in the testes of males. They have only one purpose, to transfer paternal hereditary material to the egg. They do no contribute to the nourishment of the embryo. In fish where fertilization takes place outside the body (external fertilization) both eggs and sperm are given off into the surrounding water during the mating process. Since eggs and sperm have only limited fertility, it requires a simultaneous extrusion of both sex products under often very close body contact during mating. This explains the various phases of the mating process, such as the entwining of bodies among labyrinth fishes or the twisting around the oviduct (of the female) by the anal fin of the male in *Ctenolucius hujeta*.

Within this context one must then also view the important prerequisite of male and female being able to act harmoniously during the mating ritual. There are, however, also those matings where the sex products are not given off simultaneously. In these

The male Dwarf Gourami, *Colisa lalia*, passes on its genetic traits by fertilizing the female's eggs during spawning. Photo by W. Sommer.

A mass of eggs can be seen just after they have been released by the female *Colisa lalia*. Photo by H.J. Richter.

The male *Colisa lalia* then places the eggs into the bubblenest to incubate.

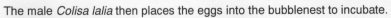

cases the female deposits her eggs first on some substrate. The male then swims closely over the (deposited) eggs and fertilizes them (e.g., cichlids, like Discus). In fish with internal fertilization, which includes all livebearers and some specialized egg-laying species (e.g., *Pseudocorynopoma)* egg and sperm cells unite inside the female's body. Initially, the copulation organ of the male transfers so-called sperm packages (spermatophores) into the body of the female. These sperm packages remain inside the oviduct of the female and remain capable of fertilizing for a long time. Therefore, females of livebearers that have been fertilized just once can produce up to 10 lots of young without a further copulation.

Simultaneously with the actual fertilization (that is, the union of sperm and egg cell) there is an

During breeding the male of the discusfish, *Symphysodon aequifasciata*, closely follows the female as she lays her eggs so that he may fertilize them shortly thereafter.

A close-up of a female discusfish, *Symphysodon aequifasciata*, laying eggs on an aquatic plant. A spawn like this may encompass 200 eggs or more.

inclusion and transfer of the carriers of hereditary material (the species specific chromosomes) into the development of the new organism. Embryonic development starts out with an increase in cell number   by cell division. During the subsequent development, and parallel to cell division, there is a relocation of nutrients into certain cells from which (eventually) specific organs develop. The egg yolk, the food supply for such organ development, is gradually used up. Just before hatching the remainder of the yolk is partially or completely absorbed into the body of the developing embryo. After the embryo releases itself from the egg shell, the content of the yolk sac provide   the first food for the young fish. The fish usually does not start to feed itself actively until after the yolk sac has been used up. Certain fish begin eating before the yolk sac has been completely absorbed. The arowanas (*Osteoglossum, Scleropages*) are examples.

PROBLEMS DURING EGG DEVELOPMENT

Experienced aquarists tend to focus their attention principally on breeding rare fish species and those which are difficult to breed. Dealing with the eggs and rearing

One of the most well-known livebearers is the Guppy, *Poecilia reticulata*. Photo by R. Zukal.

the young pose few problems for them. On the other hand, beginning aquarists prefer to care for less difficult species, and for them the problems are more likely to be in raising the young. The reason for this is a discrepancy between the limited experience and those experiences yet to be gathered in looking after eggs and young.

The embryological development taking place inside the egg is of variable duration, depending upon the individual egg laying species. It can either be reduced or delayed, depending upon external factors such as water quality and temperature. It is generally assumed that looking after the eggs in brood-caring species requires little attention. This is, however, less applicable to species from extremely mineral-poor waters with low bacterial levels. In species not exhibiting brood care the burden of attention for the eggs is fully upon the breeder. Here work efforts and problems involved increase with the duration of embryological development. Yet, we also know of notable exceptions from among the bottom-spawning (annual) killifish. In fact, we find the longest ecologically dependent embryological development period (but also relatively insensitive eggs) among some of these species.

A beautiful pair of *Pterolebias zonatus* moments before spawning. Photo by H.J. Richter.

The pair of *Pterolebias zonatus* preparing to dig down into the peat moss. Photo by H.J. Richter.

Notice how close the male and female are to each other as they dig down into the peat moss. Photo by H.J. Richter.

Let us now take a look in detail at some interesting cases and the specific problems they pose for the tropical fish breeder. Normally the eggs of annual killifish require a dry rest period (diapause) for proper embryological development. This is genetically imposed because of naturally occurring dry periods which result in a complete drying out of the habitats of these fishes. In order to survive such rest periods, the eggs of these species are protected by a special egg membrane. Typical representatives of these fish are found in the the South American genera *Austrofundulus, Cynolebias, Pterolebias, Rachovia, Terranotus*, as well as the genera *Nothobranchius, Roloffia* and *Aphyosemion* from the African continent. As a protection against desiccation and other external factors, their egg membrane is particularly strong and firm. This firmness is not achieved until some time after spawning. The required rest period is best achieved by storing the eggs in slightly damp (even dry) peat moss. The total development period of the eggs is species-specific and can last from 4 to 6 weeks, 3 to 5 months or even 6 to 9 months. The variable development period here too is influenced by external factors (oxygen supply, degree of dampness, temperature), which even affect individual eggs to a different degree. For instance, among a batch of eggs from one species there may well be individual eggs which require much longer time for their development than the majority of eggs in the same lot. Maybe this is a natural phenomenon designed to assure the survival of the species under extreme climatic conditions (continued drought conditions over long periods of time). Under captive (aquarium) conditions it is advisable to get these eggs to hatch through repeated immersion of the peat moss in pre-conditioned water. For instance, it has been reported that eggs from *Nothobranchius korthausae* were still viable after 14 months. The exact time when

Two male *Nothobranchius korthausae* sparring with each other. Photo by K. Tanaka.

A male *Nothobranchius rachovii* attempting to spawn with a female. Photo by W. Sommer.

The eggs of this *Cynolebias constanciae* will require a drying out period before they can be successfully hatched. Photo by W. Sommer.

the eggs should be immersed can be determined visually by assessing their degree of development. To do that, a few eggs are removed from the peat moss, rinsed off well and all peat particles are removed. When examining the eggs with a hand-held magnifying glass (10 to 12x magnification), the eyes of the embryo must be clearly visible as dark pigmented structures. If the eggs are immersed too early and the young still have a large yolk sac, there will be many 'belly-sliders' among them. If this is done too late there are also many young unable to swim properly and they will have a caved-in abdomen. Yet, sometimes even fully developed eggs will produce only very few young or none at all. To avoid this, here are a few hints which can be used to enhance the hatching rate:

—About 2 weeks prior to immersion increase the temperature at which the peat moss is stored (25 to 28°C).

—Immersion is done in soft, cool water (15 to 18°C), which is subsequently warmed up to 25 to

A freshly laid killifish egg in a strand of *Elodea*. Photo by N. Elder.

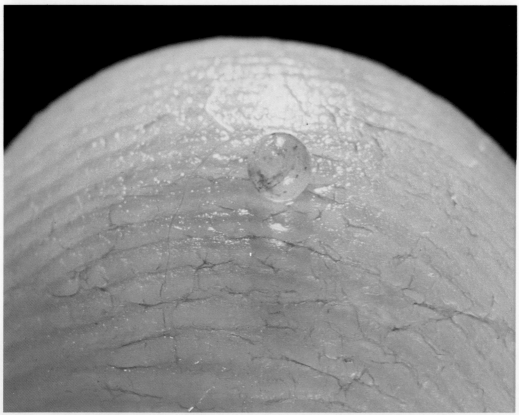

Another close-up of a freshly laid killifish egg on the tip of a person's finger. Photo by N. Elder.

A gaudily colored pair of *Nothobranchius patrizii*. Photo by W. Sommer.

27°C. It is important to make sure that the peat moss is evenly wetted and a low water level of only 5 to 6 cm is maintained.

—By giving carbon dioxide via an air hose with an air stone attached into the tank the carbon dioxide level is increased, which promotes egg hatching.

Following a slight raising of the water level, the young are scooped out and transferred to a separate rearing tank without bottom substrate. This is an opportunity to start gradually adding the first (small) volume of hard tap water to the soft hatching water. The peat moss should not be discarded but instead kept dry for another few weeks. With some effort one can also search through the peat moss for any unhatched eggs.

Because of the resistance of these eggs against fungal or bacterial infection, the breeders of bottom-spawning "annuals" must be credited more for their patience rather than for painstaking care of the eggs. Nevertheless, precise details about egg development and immersion should be recorded in order to find out the precise step-by-step breeding requirements.

Somewhat different is the situation with the spawn from sensitive tetras, barbs, non-annual killies and most small catfish. In many cases, the tiny,

It it advisable to rear the young of a spawn in a separate aquarium in order to better regulate food intake and cleanliness. Illustration by J. Quinn.

A sexually mature pair of *Corydoras aeneus*. Photo by Dr. H.J. Franke.

A pair of *Corydoras aeneus* beginning to spawn. Notice the larger female nudging the side of the male. Photo by H.J. Richter.

clear eggs are hardly visible. They are best seen when the tank is back-lit. The first decision to make is whether to leave the eggs in the spawning tank and to transfer the adults (also siphoning off any bottom debris and replacing with water of identical quality). Alternatively, the eggs can be removed with a large pipette or small siphon and transferred to another tank with identical water quality and temperature. Water plants with eggs attached and artificial spawning mops can be transferred the same way.

The eggs of small catfish (*Corydoras* species) are often attached to tank walls. From there they can be removed with a razor blade, drawn obliquely upward from below the eggs, and then transferred in the same manner as described above. Whether they are attached again to the sides of the new tank is not of any great significance. Using this procedure of egg transfer gives a good idea of the number of eggs produced at one spawning. Moreover, new pairs can be set up to spawn in the breeding tank, since the water possibly contains substances which enhance spawning. The tank containing eggs must always be kept dark, and the eggs must be closely

After much body contact, eggs are deposited on the front glass of the aquarium. Photo by H.J. Richter.

The pair of *Corydoras aeneus* continue to interact for some time after spawning has been completed. Photo by H.J. Richter.

A close-up of a batch of *Corydoras aeneus* eggs. Photo by H.J. Richter.

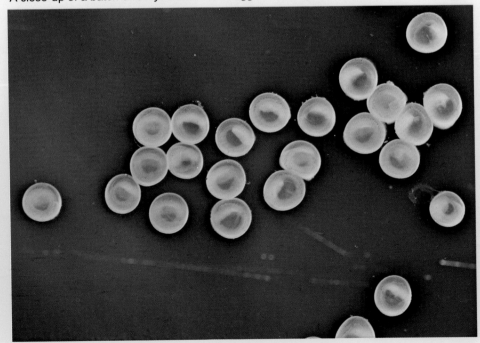

monitored. Fertilized and normally developing eggs are generally clear with a sharp peripheral outline. Unfertilized or damaged eggs are cloudy or white, and eggs covered with fungus can be recognized by the typically white (fuzzy) appearance. Dead eggs or those covered in fungus must be immediately removed with a pipette, since fungi as well as protozoans can rapidly infect adjacent healthy eggs. Unsuitable water quality, the lack of cleanliness when setting up the breeding tank, carelessness when transferring the eggs, unsuitable temperatures and too much light are the most frequent causes of

egg mortalities. Far less common would be causes related to inadequate fertilization.

Damaged eggs are quickly attacked by bacteria, which in turn favors the development of protozoans and so causes the termination of egg development. In order to prevent or at least reduce damage of this kind, many breeders use bactericidal additives (methylene blue) in the water. Also, repeated application of acriflavine (.4 to .6 g/100 liters) often leads to a die-off of protozoans. This substance must not be added earlier than about 1 to 2 hours AFTER spawning has occurred. Anti-fungal agents are

Methylene blue is an ideal anti-fungal agent used in the artificial hatching of fish eggs because it retards the growth of fungus and its spread. Photo by Dr. Herbert R. Axelrod.

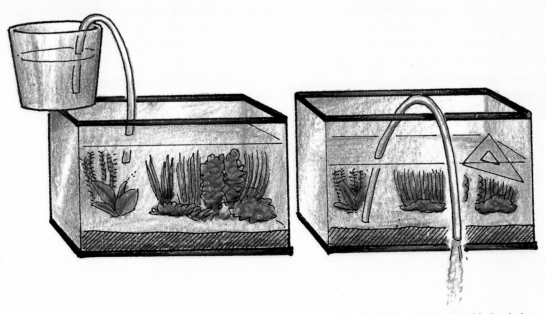

After eggs hatch and babies become free-swimming, new water of similar quality should slowly be added to replenish old nutrient-poor water as shown at left. If water is siphoned out of the fry tank (as shown at right), special care must be taken to make sure that fry are not sucked from the tank. Illustration by J. Quinn.

also available from pet shops. When using bacteriostatic agents it is important to keep in mind that the effect of these substances must always be taken in the context of the prevailing water conditions. For instance, they produce different effects in hard water with a neutral pH than in extremely soft water with a weakly acidic pH. Here too, only trial-and-error can determine the most suitable treatment in a particular situation. Once the fry have hatched it is advisable that the treated water be exchanged for new water of suitable quality. These substances can indeed have an unfavorable effect on the egg membranes and so make hatching difficult. These breeding

techniques underline how important it is to always have an adequate volume of suitable pre-conditioned water on hand.

Now let us have a look at a few less problematic cases when breeding fish. Here we are dealing with species which practice either partial or total brood care. They are fish which are recommended for the beginning aquarist, especially since they will readily breed in water of medium hardness. Little care is needed for the eggs and overall there is not much effort involved in breeding these species. They include most of the cichlids from Central and South America, as well as those from the Great Lakes of Africa's interior, with their diverse forms of brood care. Also included in this category are many labyrinth fish (mouth-brooding species as well as bubble-nest builders), as well as some loaches.

In the wild, fish progeny are most endangered during the early development stages. In order to guarantee the survival of a particular species "nature" provides either a large number of young or establishes a particular type of behavior, such as brood care, which assures minimal losses due to predation or adverse environmental influences.

Cichlids display the most well-defined type of brood care. Ichthyological ethologists distinguish between mouth

brooders and substrate spawners. Substrate spawning manifests itself initially in the selection, cleaning, and defense of the spawning site and in the caring for the eggs and young. Traditionally, aquarists look at substrate spawners as fishes that attend to their clutch of eggs, fan them, remove unfertilized or fungus-covered eggs, assist in hatching by "chewing" the fully developed eggs, guarding and frequently moving the embryos and leading and defending the (free-swimming) young.

Substrate spawning is an innate (instinctively-controlled) behavior which is triggered in adult fish by their readiness to

An extreme close-up of a *Herichthys* species laying eggs on a rock. It is shortly after this that the male will slowly glide over the eggs and release his sperm to fertilize the eggs. Photo by MP & C Piednoir.

The male *Herichthys bifasciatus* is seen here closely following the female as she lays her eggs. Photo by MP & C Piednoir.

The female *Herichthys bifasciatus* tending the newly laid eggs in order to prevent the spread of fungus. Photo by MP & C Piednoir.

breed. A successful reproductive process includes very specific behavioral manifestations and changes in coloration, as well as innately controlled types of behavior of the brood. Also acting on these processes are chemical and optical stimuli and a certain ability to learn.

If the substrate spawning behavior proceeds normally, which is generally the case with suitable matched partners and favorable environmental conditions, the aquarist hardly needs to expect any difficulties. If, however, for some reason substrate spawning is inhibited due to certain adverse influences, there can be incorrect behavior. This manifests itself by parents eating their own eggs, the embryos or even free-swimming young. In young, inexperienced pairs this may happen only during the first few breedings, thereafter which all subsequent broods are raised normally. But it can also happen that parents consistently eat their own young. Should this happen, the breeder has to act and remove the clutch of eggs and treat it as mentioned above. In fact, it is also justifiable to remove the first batch of eggs from rare and valuable species, and those from fishes that have taken a long time to breed. This is especially true of Discus

Before attempting to breed substrate-spawning fish, like these *Apistogramma agassizi*, it is vital to first wait for a pair to form naturally in order to assure a stable breeding ability. Photo by H.J. Richter.

It can also happen among mouth brooders (that is, those fish which exhibit the most refined form of brood care) that an egg-carrying female suddenly, after a few days, has an empty mouth. If, after the second or third clutch, these fish still have not yet learned to carry the eggs properly until they hatch, the breeder must secure the eggs in time to hatch them separately. It stands to reason that in these cases certain environmental reasons influence the breeding activities, but these are difficult to detect and to eliminate. Removing the eggs is possible for larger cichlids, but not from mouth-brooding labyrinth fishes such as the small (only 4 cm long) *Betta picta.* To remove the eggs, the fish is taken into one hand and held above a dish with water from the

Mouthbrooding fish, such as *Ophthalmotilapia ventralis* shown here, that spawn for the first time might not carry their eggs to full term due to being too nervous. Photo by A. Konings.

The attractively colored *Betta coccina*. Photo by H. Linke.

Attempting to remove the eggs from the mouth of this diminuitve mouthbrooder, *Betta picta*, would probably cause a great deal of injury to the fish. Photo by H.J. Richter.

aquarium. With the index finger of the other hand or a sharpened pencil, one opens the mouth of the fish gently. Shaking the fish slightly and dipping it briefly into the water will cause the fish to let go of the eggs or embryos. It is possible to remove the eggs as early as the same day of the spawning, but it is better to wait a few days into the embryonic development. Usually a female will eat her own brood only if she is harassed too much by other fish in the same tank, or unduly molested by an over-eager aquarist.

Eggs or embryos removed from the mouth are best caught in a small plastic coffee sieve or a fine-meshed hand net, which is then suspended in a small rearing tank. An airstone with a slight bubble stream is placed directly next to or underneath the sieve. Frequent monitoring and adding an anti-fungal agent to the water usually assure that there are no problems with fungus spreading over the eggs or dying embryos.

Mouthbrooding *Tropheus* species are best kept and bred in large schools. If they are caught and transferred to another tank it is not too uncommon for them to eat the young or spit out the eggs. With other mouth brooders, such as *Pseudocrenilabrus philander dispersus* which are bred in pairs or with excess females, only the

The easiest way to relieve a brooding female fish of her eggs is to use one's finger to carefully pry open the mouth and allow the fry to gently fall out into a container of water from the breeding aquarium. Photos by M. Smith.

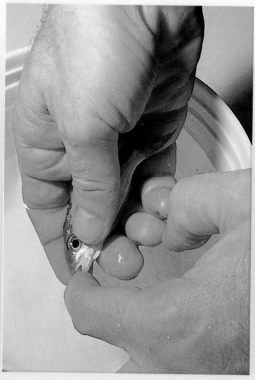
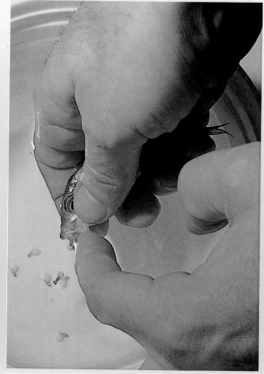

If the babies that have been removed from a brooding female have not yet completely absorbed their yolk sacs, the use of an artificial egg hatcher/tumbler may be needed to further help the embryos to develop into free-swimming babies. Photo by M. Smith.

Tropheus moorii is one mouthbrooding fish that may need to have its eggs removed and artificially reared due its nervous behavior. Photo by A. Konings.

A female *Pseudocrenilabrus philander dispersus* with her free-swimming babies. Photo by R. Zukal.

The Egyptian Mouthbrooder, *Pseudocrenilabrus multicolor*, is one of the most colorful riverine cichlids of Africa. A male **(above)** displaying to a female in the background while **(below)** a male and female are in the midst of spawning. Photos by H.J. Richter.

egg-carrying female is left in the breeding tank and the male removed. This species forms a maternal family. The female alone cares for the young after they have started to swim on their own and will still pick them up in her mouth to give them protection for a few days.

Here are a few more hints concerning mouth brooding labyrinth fish. Most of these fish are very peaceful and cryptic, and they should be left undisturbed as much as possible. Unfortunately, most of them require soft water for breeding. If such water is on

hand and at the same time a heavy plant cover is also present in the breeding tank, the outlook is good for successful breeding. If breeding is unsuccessful it is usually very difficult to come up with any specific reasons, such as inadequate water quality, disturbances or incompatibility between the partners. These fish require only a small area of about 15 x 15 cm (6 x 6") for spawning; the remainder of the tank can be overgrown with plants. If an ample number of additional *Myriophyllum* or any other dense aquatic plants are planted in the

A spawning pair of the mouthbrooding *Betta edithae*. Photo by H.J. Richter.

The aquatic plant *Myriophyllum brasiliense* will provide excellent hiding places for newly hatched young. Photo by R. Zukal.

tank, this will assure that there is adequate cover for the newly hatched young. In the mouthbrooding labyrinth fishes, as indeed in some cichlids, brood care ceases after the young are free-swimming.

In bubble nest builders one does not need to worry about the eggs, which are guarded by the male. Once spawning has been completed the female should be removed. Brood care by the male comes to an end when the young are free-swimming; he should then also be removed. If a bubble-nest must be scooped out of the tank (e.g., from a community tank) this is best done with a glass bowl. If the water level is kept low the eggs usually develop without any problems.

Brood-caring catfish males (*Sturisoma*) must be permitted to guard the eggs until they hatch. The males tend to "mouth" the eggs in order to provide development and hatching support, and must not be disturbed in this activity. Once the young have hatched they can be removed with a large pipette or siphon. If these fish spawn on the sides of a community tank, the eggs should be removed, since they would be eaten by the other fish. *Ancistrus* and *Rineloricaria* species, which prefer to spawn inside bamboo or PVC pipes, can easily be transferred into a separate rearing tank by holding both ends of the pipe shut (retaining the fish, eggs and water inside). Oxygen-rich, gently flowing water is very beneficial for the embryonic development of these eggs.

A male *Sturisoma panamense* watching over a batch of freshly laid eggs. Photo by G. Lawrence.

After Hatching Has Taken Place

Once the eggs have hatched, the yolk sac is generally used up within a few days or a couple of weeks and the young fry must be fed. This is the start of real work for the breeder. At this point he has to comply immediately with the following prerequisites:

—Securing suitable food and maintaining a feeding regimen of three to five feedings a day.

—More frequent water changes.

—Assuring optimal water temperature in the rearing tank as well as for the pre-conditioned storage water.

While the latter two points are generally easy to comply with, providing a continuous suitable food supply usually requires considerable effort. Therefore, it is imperative to explore suitable food supplies from accessible pools, ponds, pet shops and lakes *before* embarking on a breeding program. There is, of course, an inherent danger that live food from natural bodies of water contains parasites which are then introduced into the rearing tank. A breeder must be aware that the principal dietary item of young

Once these fish larvae become completely freeswimming, they will need a constant supply of quality live foods as well as clean water and a temperature to their liking. Photo by M.P. and C. Piednoir.

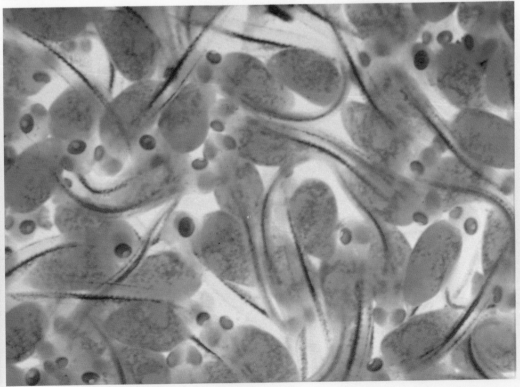

fish is live food. The equipment required to secure live food, such as fine-meshed hand nets, plankton nets, various sieves or strainers, as well as transport containers will not be discussed here in detail. Besides, they are basic tools for any dedicated aquarist. If the breeder does not have access to wild food supplies, he must inform himself about breeding food organisms and start culturing the appropriate type of food.

In order to rear healthy fish under optimal conditions, you need live food of various kinds, quality and sizes. The basic live food diet can further be supplemented with quality dried foods, which, for some species, should be rich in plant ingredients.

THE RIGHT FOOD AT THE RIGHT TIME

Before the essentials of feeding and rearing are discussed, we should first look at the most important food organisms and, where appropriate, their culture for aquarium purposes. There are books available specifically on live food production, available at your local pet dealer.

Paramecia

1) A cylindrical two-liter glass container is filled more than halfway with bundled straw or corn husks. Water is added to fill the container completely. This mixture is "seeded" with a small amount of liquid from an existing *Paramecium* culture. Alternatively, you can add some water from a pond, including a small mud

Protozoans of the genus *Paramecium* and related genera can be very useful for feeding tiny fry too small to eat baby brine shrimp. Illustrations by J. Quinn.

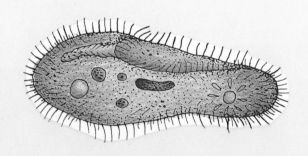

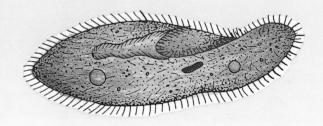

As in many other tropical fishes, these *Parambassis ranga* exhibit a lot of close body contact during spawning. Photo by J. Palicka.

The pair may be in close contact for some time before eggs are laid and fertilized. Photo by H.J. Richter.

sample (to be repeated, if required). The container should be placed in a warm location (20 to 23° C), which is bright but without direct exposure to sun light. The decaying mixture will start to smell, so it should be covered. Bacterial development will cloud the water and remove virtually all oxygen except in the uppermost water layer. Only *Paramecium,* which tends to live directly under the water surface, can survive under these conditions.

In about 2 to 3 weeks there will be a 10 mm thick layer of these ciliate protozoans along the surface. Once a peak in development (bloom) has been reached, the culture will start to deteriorate rapidly, and a new one must be started. Before *Paramecium* can be used for feeding they must be cleaned. This can be done by transferring via pipette a small volume of *Paramecium* into a test tube. A cotton plug is placed on top of the *Paramecium* mixture, and then water is added. After a few hours the *Paramecium* will have penetrated the cotton wool plug and gathered above it in the clean water. At that stage they can be fed to young fish.

2) Aquarium shops and tropical fish stores usually carry a granulate to start up infusoria cultures. This granulate can be used as per instructions included in the package, or as per method listed above, adding some of the granulate instead pond water and mud. *Paramecium* is only suitable as food for very small fish fry, and then only during their first few days. After that a larger and more nutritious type of food has to be offered.

Microworms

Microworms *(Panagrellus silusiae),* are an often-used food for small fish. Breeding these organisms requires a container

If you are able to successfully breed *Parambassis ranga*, the first food you should give the newly hatched young is microworms. Photo by H.J. Richter.

A juvenile *Metynnis fasciatus*. Photo by A. Norman.

This newly-hatched *Metynnis* species would be an ideal candidate for feeding microworms to because of its exceedingly small size. Photo by M. Shobo.

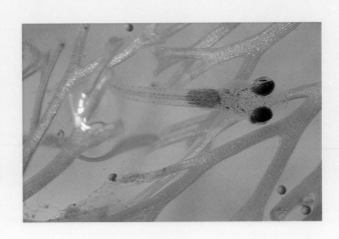

A stunning male *Aphanius mento*.
Photo by W. Sommer.

with a tightly closing lid. The bottom of the container is covered with a thin layer of dry oatmeal which is then moistened with ample milk. The medium is seeded with a small sample from an existing microworm culture and kept warm (20 to 24° C). The worms breed very rapidly and then start to crawl up the glass wall of the container. From there they can be removed (scraped off) easily with a spatula and given directly into the tank as food for young fish. Not all fish species though will eat them. The fry should be closely monitored (examined under a magnifying glass or a low microscopic magnification) to determine that the microworms are actually eaten and the young fish are really growing.

Grindal worms

This species of worm, *Enchytraeus buchholtzi*, is much smaller than the well-known white worm, *E. albidus.* It is particularly well suited as food for young fish. These worms are bred in a small, flat wooden box of at least 15 x 20 cm and 8 to 10 cm high, which is filled with boiled (sterilized), semi-moist peat moss. Starter cultures are available from tropical fish stores and aquarium shops, or possibly from aquarist friends. The starter culture is placed at the bottom of a small depression in the peat moss and is then covered with a tablespoon of cooked oatmeal. The depression is then covered with a thin layer of peat moss. This box is to be kept in a warm but damp place. When, after a few weeks, the

This juvenile *Cyprichromis leptosoma* is adapted to picking out small live foods in the water such as microworms and grindal worms. Photo by H. Mayer.

Even as an adult this elegant South American dwarf cichlid, *Apistogramma cacatuoides,* would enjoy feedings of grindal worms. Photo by H.J. Richter.

worms have adequately multiplied, the first few lots can be removed for feeding to the fish. Worms are easier to remove when the entire surface area inside the box is covered with a neatly fitting piece of window glass. The worms then tend to stick to the underside of the glass. Separate grindal worm cultures should be started at different intervals, so that when one culture is used for feeding, the worms in the other have an opportunity to reproduce. Operating two to three cultures simultaneously will usually suffice to cover all dietary needs of the fish. Grindal worms are highly nutritious, but they must not be the exclusive diet for fish.

Baby brine shrimp

Nauplii of crustaceans of the genus *Artemia* are among the most popular fish foods for young growing fish. They are also quite suitable for most other fish. Only very few newly hatched fish need, at first, *Paramecium* or rotifers before they are large enough to feed on the larger *Artemia* nauplii. These small crustaceans are easily raised from eggs available from all aquarium and tropical fish stores. The enormous advantage of *Artemia* nauplii lies in the fact that they can be hatched quickly, neatly timed to when they are required to be fed as the first food for newly hatched fish. Moreover, the work involved

A large school of *Cyprichromis leptosoma* of all sizes would enjoy regular helpings of baby brine shrimp as a supplement to their diet. Photo by H. Mayer.

A simple diagram of procedures required to hatch *Artemia* nauplii, or baby brine shrimp, from eggs all the way to feeding them to one's fish. Illustrations by J. Quinn.

in hatching *Artemia* is insignificant. A small portion (¼ to 1 tsp) of *Artemia* eggs is added to one liter of seawater (15-20 g of non-iodized household salt or regular sea salt) in a wide-necked bottle. This mixture is then heavily aerated, so that the eggs are kept constantly stirred up. The water temperature should be at about 24 to 26° C. The nauplii will start hatching in about 24 hours. When the aeration is turned off any unhatched eggs and empty egg shells will settle to the bottom. The newly hatched nauplii can then easily be drawn off. If aeration is resumed the remaining eggs will hatch progressively and more nauplii

can be removed after another 12 to 24 hours. These tiny food organisms can survive without food in seawater for several days, but they will die off relatively fast when put into freshwater. Therefore, *Artemia* nauplii should only be fed in small amounts (which are quickly eaten), several times a day.

Rotifers

Rotifers (Rotataria) because of their small size (.1 to .2 mm) are ideally suited for feeding young fish, principally for newly hatched fish. Rotifers can be caught in quiet ponds and similar bodies of water using plankton (fine mesh) nets. Periodically rotifers can

San Francisco Bay Brand markets both *Artemia* eggs and the equipment and supplies used in their efficient hatching.

The young are clearly visible in the throat sac of this *Cyprichromis leptosoma* female. At this stage, the young are ready to come out and begin feeding on rotifers and baby brine shrimp. Photo by H. Mayer.

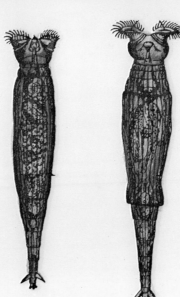

Typical rotifers. These tiny live foods are great for extremely small baby fish. Illustrations by J. Quinn.

occur in huge aggregations, or they may be totally absent for prolonged periods of time. Apart from free-swimming rotifers, there are also often sessile (attached) rotifers. In a plankton net, rotifers separate out as slimy, usually reddish brown layers on the sides and bottom of the net. In a jar, rotifers form slowly moving "clouds." Examining samples from such a cloud under 5 to 10 times magnification, you can see that these tiny organisms are indeed present. They should be transported in the water in cans, plastic containers, etc. These must be stored in a cool place. Crowded rotifers can live only a short period of time, but in lower densities they can be kept for a few days. When frozen they are ideally suited for some juvenile loricariid catfish. Possible by-catches of nauplii from copepods or other larger crustaceans should be separated from rotifers by pouring the entire rotifer transport water through appropriately fine sieves.

Crustaceans

Aquarists are familiar with a number of crustaceans which are

A sub-adult *Pterygoplichthys gibbiceps*. Once this catfish has been weaned off of rotifers, a diet high in vegetable matter is recommended. Photo by B. Kahl.

An undescribed *Peckoltia* species that should also be given rotifers when very young. Photo by B. Kahl.

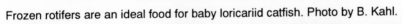

Frozen rotifers are an ideal food for baby loricariid catfish. Photo by B. Kahl.

often used as fish food. These include the well-known freshwater crustaceans *Cyclops* (copepods) and *Daphnia*, better known as water fleas (phyllopods). In their various developmental and growth stages they form the main stay of proper fish nutrition. Cyclops nauplii are, apart from rotifers, the best food for young fish. In size, the smallest cyclops nauplii are distinctly smaller than the smallest nauplii of *Artemia salina*. Depending upon the nutrients in the pond, cyclops nauplii are grayish, greenish or even orange-red in color. They, too, have to be caught in very fine-meshed nets, to be further separated into different sizes by sifting them through sieves. Particularly popular with breeders are the nauplii of *Diaptomus*. These are less active so that slower moving fry, like *Parambassis ranga*, can catch them much easier. Once cyclops nauplii have reached their advanced developmental stage, or

A popular crustacean used as food for fish is *Daphnia pulex*. Illustration by J. Quinn.

Nothobranchius eggersi. Photo by K. Tanaka.

Rotifers (upper 3 figures) and the nauplii of the crustacean *Cyclops* (lower figure) are used by aquarists as food for their fry. Illustration by J. Quinn.

These baby Buffalo Heads, *Steatocranus casuarius*, will grow faster on live foods than on dry foods alone. Photo by J. Winco.

The protrusible mouth on this *Cyprichromis leptosoma* is testimony to its ability to suck up small live foods at an adult size. Photo by A. Konings.

as adults, they can be potentially dangerous to very small fish by actively attacking them. If too many nauplii are given at any one time into a warm tank they can rapidly reach the predatory stage and so cause considerable damage among fish fry. Therefore, the best rule is to feed several times per day, but always in small quantities.

Water fleas of the genera *Daphnia* and *Bosmina* are also valuable fish food. Although they are less nutritious than cyclops, water fleas are an almost indispensable dietary supplement for tropical fish. These small crustaceans can also be subdivided into different size categories, which makes it easy to feed them to young fish at different stages in their development. *Daphnia* can also be easily frozen, which makes them

an excellent food reserve. Frozen fish food must also be given in small amounts. In order to avoid gastro-intestinal problems it is important to feed only frozen food which has been thoroughly thawed out! Frozen food can be further enhanced with (commercially available) vitamin supplements. All uneaten food in a rearing tank must be siphoned out as quickly as possible.

Merely providing the correct food and then feeding it is not all there is to breeding fish. In addition, the breeder must determine the correct time for particular foods, and he must control and monitor that the food is actually eaten by the fish. References to feeding free-swimming fish fry does not mean that the fish are actually swimming about openly in the tank. Many of the young cling to

This wild-caught *Julidochromis transcriptus* will thrive on a diet that includes daphnia in its menu. Photo by M. Smith.

The young of *Cyathopharynx furcifer* will eagerly accept a variety of small live foods such as daphnia and baby brine shrimp. Photo by MP &C Piednoir.

A sleeper goby, *Eleotris labretonis,* that would also appreciate the addition of live foods into its diet, especially when young. Photo by W. Sommer.

A magnificent spawning pair of *Herichthys managuense*. Photo by MP & C Piednoir.

the tank walls or to the water surface, others hide among the plants. The breeder has to look at them carefully to check whether the yolk sac has been fully absorbed. Young capable of swimming will dart rapidly about when disturbed and seek cover actively. This is a sure sign that they must be fed. To be on the safe side, it is better to offer a size of food which is somewhat smaller than seems required. Anyone breeding fish for the first time and examining the young closely will be amazed at how small the food must be for the young of labyrinth fishes, rainbow fishes and some of the very small tetras, to be able to eat it. Whether the fry can handle the food or not can be seen only by their bulging (or empty) abdomens.

Generally, young fish go looking for food and in doing so move through the entire tank. But there are also those species where the young withdraw into a dark corner and remain there, while the food organisms are attracted towards the light. In these cases the sides of the tank should be covered in order to establish different tank sections by changing the direction of incoming light. This forces the young fish as well as the food organisms to frequently change sites whereby they are bound to encounter each other.

For fish fry that remain primarily at the surface, we use an airstone or a circulating pump, creating a current which continuously moves food organisms toward the surface. Surface-oriented fish like to maintain their position in a slight water current and will snap up passing food organisms.

One can readily ascertain whether baby fish are healthy and eating properly by the presence of their greatly extended bellies. Photo by U. Werner.

The young of the Threadfin Rainbowfish, *Iriatherina werneri*, tend to congregate near the surface of the water; consequently, food should be offered at the surface. Photo by H.J. Richter.

The same can be said for the young of this Australian rainbowfish *Melanotaenia splendida australis*. Photo by G. Allen.

Concurrent with the growth of the young fish also comes the need for a change in food organisms and where to get the new food. There is an advantage in this, since a uniform diet would have detrimental effects on the health of a fish. Therefore, it is advisable to supplement even a variable diet of live food with finely ground dried foods provided the young have grown to about 10 to 12 mm. In fact, dried food with a large plant material component is absolutely essential for rearing livebearers, loricariid catfish and some tetras.

THE EFFECT OF WATER CHANGE AND TEMPERATURE ON GROWTH

The importance of water changes for the care of the brood stock has already been emphasized; it becomes even more important for rearing the young. This can best be illustrated with an example. The Blunt-nosed Gar, *Ctenolucius hujeta,* produces up to 2,000 eggs at one spawning. A large percentage of the young can be reared. When properly fed these young grow so rapidly that within 8 weeks they can reach a size of 7 to 8 cm. Such growth requires 3 to 4 daily feedings of live food.

In order to raise the young of any species of tropical fish, including this *Eleotris labretonis*, one should provide three to four feedings daily with careful monitoring of the water quality through water changes in order to rid the tank of excess waste products. Photo by W. Sommer.

Starting out with cyclops nauplii followed by fully developed cyclops and daphnia, followed by white and black mosquito larvae, house flies and tubifex, an incredible biomass is added to the tank which is eaten and digested. It is not difficult to imagine the amount of visible and invisible excretions that are produced. It can best be judged by the amount of food required. Apart from the obvious logistic problems (securing ever-growing live food supplies, the need for additional rearing tanks, etc.), water changes play an equally important role in the growth of these young. If frequent water changes are omitted, the fish will soon swim in

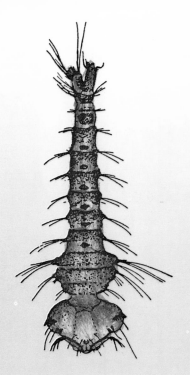

Mosquito larvae **(left)** are an excellent food for young that have put on a little size as well as for adults. Tubifex worms **(above)** are also excellent food for young fish and adults alike. Illustration by J. Quinn. Photo by I. Francais.

their own excrement. It is not difficult to imagine the stress and harm to which this would expose the fish.

Although not all fish species undergo such incredibly rapid growth, the problems associated with metabolism and the removal of metabolic waste products remain one of the major tasks of a fish breeder. This is also a prerequisite for getting healthy fish progeny. Any negligence on the part of the breeder will result in poor growth and susceptibility to disease among the young.

Epiplatys chaperi requires a well balanced diet of live, prepared and freeze-dried foods with an emphasis on live foods for the youngsters. Photo by W. Sommer.

A variety of prepared foods. Freeze-dried blood worms and plankton (left) and powdered foods (right). Photos by I. Francais.

A female *Nanochromis squamiceps* leading her babies around in search of food. Photo by H. Linke.

It is difficult to give explicit details in regard to frequency and volume of water changes. This is very much dependent upon individual situations and the breeder's ability to assess these correctly and in time. If water changes cause problems one would expect an unsuitable water quality to be the cause. It need

A beautiful and seldom seen killifish, *Procatopus aberrans*. Careful management of the water quality is vital in order to keep the young of this fish alive and in good health. Photo by W. Sommer.

not be reiterated that any make-up water must be free of chlorine gas and have been suitably preconditioned, unless slow drips of fresh water can be added almost continuously via a water changer available at most pet shops.

If a particular batch of young have been bred in soft water, subsequent water changes should only very gradually increase water hardness. Fry raised in that manner tend to be much less sensitive later on when exposed to variable water conditions in other tanks.

Generally, young fish should be kept somewhat warmer during the first few days after hatching. Of course, the specific temperature requirements of individual species have to be taken into consideration. Barbs, labyrinth fishes, some killifish (those living close to the surface) and rainbow fish should be given a temperature of around 30° C. Some of the tetras, young loricariid catfish and those of the genus *Corydoras* (which all need high oxygen levels) prefer a rearing temperature about 4 to 5° C lower. In essence, every breeder must gather his own experiences in this area; he or she must study the literature and then draw the required conclusions as they apply to their own particular breeding program.

Nanochromis parilus is a soft water-loving fish whose babies will also need soft water if they are to grow up and mature properly. Photo by W. Sommer.

Practical Fish Breeding

Every aquarist should closely document any deliberately planned breeding attempt, especially when it is successful. It is sufficient to record the most essential data (water quality, temperature, food organism cultures), step-by-step description of techniques used as well as any other breeding details. When completed, it should be evaluated and the appropriate conclusions drawn in respect to future breeding of particular species.

A pair of *Herichthys maculicauda* in the act of breeding. Photo by R. Stawikowski.

THE BREEDING PROTOCOL
SOUTH AFRICAN
MOUTHBROODER,
*Pseudocrenilabrus philander
dispersus*

May 25th: Purchased 7 juveniles from Murray's Petshop.

Size: 30 to 35 mm, sex unknown.

to June 1st: Kept in quarantine tank 10 gallon (40 L), tap water (total hardness 16° dH, carbonate hardness 3°).

Diet: *Daphnia*, cyclops (fish healthy).

June 2nd: Transferred to community tank with Boeseman's Rainbowfish, *Melanotaenia boesemani*, Silverdollars and Dwarf Gouramies.

Tap water, pH neutral, 24 to 29° C (variable), power filter.

July 5th: Sex distribution: 1 larger male, about 50 mm, 3 smaller males, about 40 to 45 mm, 3 females, about 35, 40 and 45 mm. Large male dominant!

Supplementary diet: Black mosquito larva, tubifex worms, dried food eagerly taken.

A pair of *Pseudocrenilabrus philander dispersus* in the process of breeding. Photo by H.J. Richter.

Another view of *Pseudocrenilabrus philander dispersus* during breeding. Photo by H.J. Richter.

These Boeseman's Rainbowfish, *Melanotaenia boesemani,* make ideal tank mates for small mouthbrooding cichlids. Photo by H.J. Richter.

August 19th: 3 females starting to get gravid; the smallest female with "caved in" abdomen.

20 August : Preparing breeding tank 70 x 35 x 35 cm, bottom substrate dark river sand, 4-6 cm thick layer. Foreground a piece of slate.

Planting: Back of the tank densely planted with Congo Fern, Java Fern and 2 Amazon sword plants (2 separate planters).

Tap water: 16 dH total hardness, 3° carbonate hardness, pH 7.2, temperature 26° C, power filter, medium filter wool and activated charcoal.

August 21st: Introduced breeding fish. 1 male about 70 mm, 1 female about 65 mm, 1 female about 60 mm.

Diet: Mosquito larvae, *Daphnia*.

August 25th: Small females hiding among plants, gular (throat) sac strongly inflated. Spawning could not be observed. Since the other fish harassed this female they were returned to the community tank.

August 25th: 30 % water change. Egg-carrying female refuses all food.

The female *Pseudocrenilabrus philander dispersus* on the verge of laying another egg. Photo by H.J. Richter.

The male *Pseudocrenilabrus philander dispersus* turns around to fertilize the eggs that the female just laid. Photo by H.J. Richter.

After the spawning has been completed, the female leaves the male's territory to incubate the eggs on her own. Photo by H.J. Richter.

September 6th: Sometimes the outline of juveniles can be seen through the skin of the gular sac.

September 8th: Started *Artemia* culture from eggs.

September 8th: Female releases young from mouth for the first time (about 25 to 30 young).

September 9th: First feeding with artemia nauplii.

September 11th: Feeding with *Artemia* nauplii/water change about 25%.

September 14th: At night the young are no longer taken into the mouth; they remain scattered along the bottom. Female transferred back to community tank.

September 15th: Water change, about 25%.

September 24th: Water change about 25%, counted 29 young, about 10 to 12 mm long.

An example of how alternating supplies of baby brine shrimp hatchers should be set up. Photo by B. Degen.

Recommended Species For The First Breeding Attempts

The following species recommended below for first breeding attempts represent very few of the large number of well-known and popular tropical fish which could also be used. When selecting these species emphasis was placed on those which are easy to breed and which do not make excessive demands in regard to water quality and food requirements. Another selection criterion was their interesting behavior and their suitability to enable the beginning aquarist to learn how to breed fish in a progressive and systematic manner.

An attractive community aquarium with tropical fishes—but they're not alll easy to spawn! Photo by B. Kahl.

LIVEBEARERS

Giving birth to live young is typical for the following, aquaristically interesting fish families:

Guppies, Swordtails, Platies, Mollies (Poeciilidae)

Highland Livebearers (Goodeidae)

Halfbeaks (Hemirhamphidae)

Four-eyes (Anablepidae)

Apart from the popular Guppies, Mollies and Platies, the family Poeciliidae also includes a large number of other interesting aquarium fish. Some of these species are ideally suited for initial breeding trials, and captive breeding would also support the conservation of these species in the wild. These are wild forms which are not common in the hobby. Some recommended livebearers are: Atoyac Swordtail, *Xiphophorus andersi*; Dwarf Swordtail, *X. pygmaeus*; Little Swordtail, *X. nigrenis*; Montezuma's Swordtail, *X. montezumae*; and Northern Platy, *X. gordoni*.

An attractive strain of Swordtail, *Xiphophorus helleri*. Photo by E. Taylor.

The Platy,
*Xiphophorus
maculatus.* Photo by
B. Kahl.

Another beautiful
Platy, *Xiphophorus
maculatus.* Photo by
B. Kahl.

The Dwarf
Swordtail,
*Xiphophorus
pygmaeus.* Photo
by L. Wischnath.

All species are easily bred, yet they are rarely ever available in the tropical fish trade; therefore, it may be necessary to contact relevant specialist organizations. Additional recommended species are *Poecilia melanogaster, P. nigrofasciata, P. dominicensis*, as well as *Priapella intermedia*.

Nearly all livebearers prefer water of medium hardness with a neutral pH value. Some require higher temperatures, others prefer a lower range (refer to the relevant literature). Poecilids must be given a vegetarian supplement to their diet (plant flakes). Those aquarists particularly interested in livebearers will find the breeding of halfbeaks especially interesting. Recommended are species of the genera *Dermogenys* and *Nomorhamphus*. Any breeding success with these fish is very much dependent upon a suitable diet. Halfbeaks are preferentially insect feeders. In captivity they should be given black mosquito larvae, fly pupae, fruit flies and some dried food. Halfbeaks prefer a floating plant cover and a slight water current. The species listed, as well as other livebearers, are particularly recommended for those aquarists who have no regular access to live food. All of these fish can be bred and reared with live brine shrimp, fruit flies and commercially available freeze-dried and dried foods.

A recently developed strain of *Poecilia sphenops*, referred to as the Gold Dust Molly. Photo by MP & C Piednoir.

TETRAS

Most tetras are open water spawners. Eggs and sperm are given off from within a school of these fish, or a pair may leave the school briefly to deposit eggs among plants, or just below the water surface. When judged in context with water requirements, breeding tetras can involve a variable degree of difficulty. Therefore, for the beginning aquarist there are really only a few species available which are easily bred and which will give the breeder practical breeding experience. The species listed below can be spawned and reared in water of medium hardness.

Aphyocharax rubropinnis,
Bloodfin. Spawns in small schools with an excess of males. Egg predator!

Gymnocorymbus ternetzi, Black Tetra. Spawns in small schools with an excess of males; must be kept well fed, otherwise an egg predator.

Hemigrammus caudovittatus, Buenos Aires Tetra. Spawns in pairs or in a small school. Requires a large spawning tank of 75 to 80 cm length, temperature 20 to 23° C. Herbivore (needs plant diet).

Hyphessobrycon flammeus, Flame Tetra. Spawns in pairs, temperature 20 to 24°C. When rearing young some plant food must also be given.

The Red-eye Tetra, *Moenkhausia sanctaefilomenae*, would be an ideal fish for a beginner's first efforts at breeding egglayers. Photo by A. Norman.

A lively group of Bloodfin Tetras, *Aphyocharax rubropinnis*. Photo by B. Kahl.

Moenkhausia sanctaefilomenae, Red-eyed Tetra. Prolific egg producer when given plant food diet. Will spawn in small schools with an excess of males. The spawning tank should be at least 60 cm long. The young will grow rapidly.

BARBS AND RELATED CARP-LIKE FISHES

As a form of colloquialism, aquarists invariably (and wrongly) describe the carp-like fishes of the family Cyprinidae as barbs. This is only mentioned here for a better understanding of this large and complex fish family.

Most small cyprinids commonly kept by aquarists are also regularly bred in captivity. Breeding behavior is generally similar within the entire family. Usually experiences gained with one species can also be applied to other species. Cyprinids always live in groups or schools. Breeding males and females will pair up from within the school, a fact which the breeder must keep in mind. Consequently, raising a number of young cyprinids from juveniles to sexual maturity is the best guarantee for getting suitably matched breeding pairs. The species listed below are suited for less experienced aquarists to gain familiarity with breeding cyprinids.

Puntius conchonius, Rosy Barb. Bottom of spawning tank must be covered with small pebbles. Water to 20° total hardness, temperature 27 to 29° C.

Tanichthys albonubes, White Cloud Mountain Minnow and *Brachydanio rerio,* Zebra Danio. Both species are easily bred in

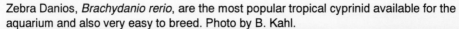

Zebra Danios, *Brachydanio rerio*, are the most popular tropical cyprinid available for the aquarium and also very easy to breed. Photo by B. Kahl.

A small school of Harlequin Rasboras, *Rasbora heteromorpha*. Photo by B. Kahl.

The Rosy Barb, *Puntius conchonius*, is another popular cyprinid readily available and easy to breed. Photo by A. Roth.

long tanks with lots of *Myriophyllum*. Temperature 20 to 22° C (2 - 3° higher for *B. rerio*). The young can be reared with live and dried foods.

Rasbora heteromorpha, Harlequin Rasbora. Places somewhat higher demands on water quality. Soft water (less than 10 degrees total hardness) and special care required. Prefers to spawn on the underside of *Cryptocoryne* leaves. Not every pair will spawn; change male or female. Temperature 25 to 28° C.

CATFISH

Since many new species of catfish have been discovered and imported during recent years, these fish are among the most popular aquarium fish. In fact, dedicated catfish specialists have had some spectacular breeding successes. Many attractive and rare *Corydoras* species have been bred, as well as members of *Brochis* and *Dianema* and some rare *Synodontis* species. Moreover, breeding successes with loricariids have been quite stabilized. The list of breeding successes is headed by *Sturisoma nigrirostrum* and *S. panamense* as well as *Farlowella* species. Captive-bred *Ancistrus* and *Rineloricaria* species are regularly available in aquarium shops. These two can be included in the list of recommended species for less experienced fish breeders. These species are often kept in community tanks as algae cleaners. When conditioned on additional plant food tablets and lettuce leaves (briefly dipped into boiling water), they tend to spawn quite willingly on bamboo rods or

Corydoras catfish are among the easiest catfish to breed in the aquarium. Depicted here is a *Corydoras panda*. Photo by H.J. Franke.

Synodontis multipunctatus was the first catfish of its genus to be bred in captivity. Photo by B. Kahl.

Rineloricaria castroi, which belongs to the family Loricariidae, is another catfish that has been bred in captivity. Photo by W. Foersch.

PVC pipes placed into the tank. The males are permitted to guard the eggs until just prior to hatching and then the entire spawning tube is transferred into a separate rearing tank.

The only problem remaining is getting suitably small food for the newly hatched young. Rotifers combined with a dried plant food or possibly hard-boiled egg yolk will help the breeder to overcome these first hurdles. Beyond that, raising the young catfish requires submerged wood (for rasping) and lettuce leaves (briefly dipped into boiling water). Any budding catfish breeder should start out with *Ancistrus* and *Rineloricaria* species.

KILLIFISH

Among the killifish there are a few species with which fish breeding becomes a real event. For instance, the American Flagfish, *Jordanella floridae*, displays some unusual types of behavior one would not expect in this fish (onset of courtship, guarding the eggs). Sub-adults can even be raised in an outdoor pond. Another killifish from Florida, *Lucania goodei*, is similarly suitable for initial breeding attempts. When kept in outdoor ponds

The Florida Bluefin, *Lucania goodei*, is a small undemanding killifish that is ideal for the beginning aquarist to start out with. Photo by W. Sommer.

A male *Rivulus cylindraceus*. Photo by K. Tanaka.

Aphyosemion striatum. Photo by K. Tanaka.

Fundulus notatus. Photo by E. Taylor.

during the summer months these fish will grow to particularly robust and colorful individuals. These species are easily bred in medium hard water with a neutral pH.

The genus *Rivulus* also offers some attractive and easily bred species for the beginning breeder. The almost perpetual spawning of species like *Rivulus cylindraceus*,

R. hartii, R. holmiae and *R. urophthalmus* is hard to stop. From among the large genus *Aphyosemion*, the easiest species are some of the non-annual forms, including *Aphyosemion australe, A. bivittatum, A. bualanum, A. gardneri* and *A. striatum.* Good breeding successes with these spectacularly colored fish are essentially guaranteed in medium hard water and with the use of peat moss filtration. If an aquarist has mainly soft water at his disposal, he may wish to try his hand at a species which produces both annually as well as non-annually. Most notable among these are *Aphyosemion calliurum, A. arnoldi, A. filamentosum* and *A. gulare.* These offer a good learning experience for later attempts with the more extreme annual forms. From among the exclusive annual forms, the beginning breeder is advised to try his hand with the popular *Nothobranchius guentheri.* There are stable aquarium populations around of this East African annual fish, which can be kept in medium hard water and will breed in somewhat softer water.

Aphyosemion gardneri is a great beginner's killifish due to its hardiness and ease of breeding. Photo by K. Tanaka.

A beautiful *Nothobranchius melanospilus.* Photo by E. Taylor.

The Chocolate Gourami, *Sphaerichthys osphromenoides*, caught in the act of breeding. Photo by H.J. Richter.

LABYRINTH FISHES

Most members of this group can easily be bred, with the exception of a few sensitive species, such as *Sphaerichthys osphromenoides* or the *Parosphromenus* species. Even though the reader will find only three species suggested here for initial breeding attempts, there are good reasons for this. It is totally sufficient to provide optimum care and to observe in detail the courtship, mating behavior and brood care of the bubble nest builder Pearl Gourami, *Trichogaster leeri*; Dwarf Gourami, *Colisa lalia*; and Betta, *Betta splendens*, and to rear the young of these three species. This then provides the basic knowledge for breeding most other labyrinth fishes. The species mentioned above are very quiet fish which display their breeding behavior in slow, deliberate movements and with a rare distinctiveness. It is also important to raise at least some of the progeny from all three species to adulthood.

A male Thick-lipped Gourami, *Colisa labiosa*. Photo by W. Sommer.

CICHLIDS

Cichlids appear to be the preferred fish by most aquarists who want to breed fish. This is due to the general popularity of their exquisite coloration and even more because of their well-defined brood care behavior. A contributing factor is that brood care behavior also assures, to a large degree, breeding success. But even in this fish family there are, of course, species which have proven to be rather difficult even for experienced fish breeders. These are primarily from soft water regions. Inexperienced fish breeders should start out with some of the small Lake Tanganyika cichlids, especially the *Julidochromis* species and various representatives of the genera *Neolamprologus* and *Telmatochromis*. And anyone wanting to breed cichlids should not omit the Rainbow Cichlid, *Herotilapia multispinosa*, as well as members of the genus *Herichthys*.

Telmatochromis brichardi from Lake Tanganyika is a recommended cichlid for the beginning tropical fish breeder to work with. Photo by W. Sommer.

A breeding pair of *Nanochromis parilus*. Notice the extended abdomen of the female indicating that she is full of eggs and ready to breed. Photo by W. Sommer.

This *Herichthys maculicauda* will require a large aquarium if one wishes to breed it since it can grow to a size of about 15 inches (45 cm). Photo by MP & C Piednoir.

Most suitable among the mouthbrooding forms are *Pseudocrenilabrus* species as well as some of the *Chromidotilapia, Labidochromis, Pseudotropheus* and *Melanochromis.* All of these have proven to be very reliable brood-caring parents. It is indeed an exciting experience to observe the dedicated parental care of the young.

Those aquarists who have access to soft water should concentrate their breeding efforts on popular dwarf cichlids (e.g., *Apistogramma, Microgeophagus* and *Pelvicachromis*). With these species it is important to use breeding pairs originating from well established stock which has already been bred in captivity for many years. Beginning aquarists are cautioned against immediately chasing after rarities.

Petrotilapia sp. "Black Flank" is a mouthbrooding cichlid with a somewhat more aggressive temperament than most other mouthbrooding fishes. Photo by A. Konings.

One of the most popular, easy to breed and readily available mouthbrooding cichlids is *Melanochromis auratus*. Photo by MP & C Piednoir.

A gorgeous male *Pelvicachromis pulcher*. Photo by MP & C Piednoir.

Dicrossus maculata is a very seldom seen species of dwarf cichlid. Photo by H.J. Richter.

A male featherfin cichlid *Ophthalmotilapia ventralis*. Photo by MP & C Piednoir.

The Cuban Cichlid, *Herichthys tetracanthus,* is one of the more aggressive cichlids to work with and as such should not be maintained unless one has some experience with large, aggressive cichlids. Photo by D. Conkel.

A dominant male *Labidochromis chisumulae*. This is an ideal cichlid to breed in small aquariums. Photo by MP & C Piednoir.

This pair of *Laetacara curviceps* is also ideally suited to breed in small aquariums because of their small size. Photo by MP & C Piednoir.

OTHER FISH SPECIES

In this category we should focus our attention on rainbowfishes and gobies. Anyone wanting to breed the colorful rainbowfishes should start out with medium hard water at a neutral pH. Such water is particularly suitable for the slow-growing young of these species. It has not yet been shown conclusively that some rainbowfish species can only be bred in soft, slightly acid water. At best, this can really only be applicable to wild caught fishes. The key problem when breeding rainbowfishes is getting suitable food for the very small young (rotifers, *Paramecium*, small copepod nauplii, powdered food for egg-laying species, etc.). Such food must be given for a relatively long period of time. Ideally suited for beginning breeders are all *Melanotaenia* species, as well as *Glossolepis incisus* and *Iriatherina werneri*. In addition, closely related species, such as *Pseudomugil signifer* and *Telmatherina ladigesi*, are also recommended for beginners.

From among the many gobies there are two species that virtually guarantee breeding success. These are the Desert Goby, *Chlamydogobius eremius*, and the Pastel Goby, *Tateurndina ocellicauda*. These two species will breed without any problems in hard water.

The Pastel Goby, *Tateurndina ocellicauda*, is one of the easiest gobies to breed in captivity. Photo by H.J. Richter.

A spawning pair of *Telmatherina ladigesi*. Photo by H.J. Richter.

Closely related to true rainbowfishes are these *Pseudomugil gertrudae*. Photo by G. Schmida.

The majestic *Popondichthys furcata* from New Guinea. Photo by G. Schmida.

The Fascination of Breeding Aquarium Fish

This book, with over 440 pages and over 500 full-color photos, is devoted to covering all major aspects of tropical freshwater fish reproduction in the aquarium. The coupling of beautiful color photos from world renowned photographers depicting fish as they are actually breeding with the profound experiences of the author has truly created a book of unique value and interest. This commanding book is a must for all who are involved in the wonderment of breeding tropical fish in captivity.

Index